HOMEWORK EDUCATION
A Powerful Tool of Learning

Arbind Kumar Jha

ATLANTIC®
PUBLISHERS & DISTRIBUTORS

Published by
ATLANTIC®
PUBLISHERS & DISTRIBUTORS
B-2, Vishal Enclave, Opp. Rajouri Garden,
New Delhi-110027
Phones : 25413460, 25429987, 25466842

Sales Office
7/22, Ansari Road, Darya Ganj,
New Delhi-110002
Phones : 23273880, 23275880, 23280451
Fax : 91-11-23285873
web : www.atlanticbooks.com
e-mail : info@atlanticbooks.com

ISBN 81-269-0647-2

Printed in India
at Nice Printing Press, Delhi

Dedicated to

All my students
Who take active part
In countless "Learning to Learn" classroom sessions
Which I love to call sessions of "Cognitive Dances".

PREFACE

The curricular transactions need various techniques to *define, expound, elucidate, generalise, verify, apply* and even *reflect* upon, the knowledge created, generated and constructed therein. Homework can be used as one of such techniques as it has all the essential ingredients in it to make curriculum transaction possible without any hitch or glitch. Moreover, by and large educationists agree that Homework Education can provide guided lives for pedagogy, which can bring about substantial change in the art and science of teaching.

More recently, research outcomes have confirmed that home assignments as a tool and technique has all the capable potential to provide not only some sound theoretical learning experiences but also practical and meaningful experiences which can make the students learning to learn. It has been rightly called the *instrument* of intellectual development with the wealth of conceptual as well as procedural rules of learning it provides. Its acceptance in the arena of school education has made a significant contribution to the pursuit of making teaching effective and learning creative. If it is used scientifically, it can bring a number of personal qualities essential for personality development. It can be stated categorically that homework as the foremost and powerful tool of learning experience has enough potentiality to enrich the purpose and process of education.

From the perspective of classroom teaching and learning, homework enables children to cover topics taught more thoroughly and with greater speed and accuracy and so that the activity of self-study becomes a natural complement of teaching. It helps both teacher and pupils to see if what has been taught have been understood fully or not. In a way it creates a dialogue between teachers and students. A teacher can examine the pupil's work in depth to find out their strength and weaknesses and make comments and give guidance to correct and help them.

Homework is a great predictor of success at any level of education — primary, secondary, senior secondary etc. If students want to achieve good percentage of marks or grades, it is important for the students to have higher competition rate on homework. The more homework students complete, especially from class six to twelve, the better they do in school according to research conducted by psychologists Harris Cooper, James J. Lindsay and Scott Greathouse (1998) of the University of Missouri — Columbia and psychologist Barbara Nye, of Tennessee State University.

Homework assignments can have many benefits for students, which they can use in their adult life. Homework can help students develop study skills that will be of value even after they leave school. It can teach them that learning takes place anywhere, not just inside the classroom. Homework can benefit children in more general ways as well. An organized homework programme helps students to gain the appropriate skills and staying power that will assist them to pole vault the challenges faced by the students during the schooling period. Also, it can foster many positive character traits, which are helpful in leading life successfully in various areas. It provides an opportunity for development of self-confidence and self-motivation — the vital components of one's personality.

Many questions and concerns arise in our mind regarding Homework. Some vital questions are following:

- Why do teachers give homework?

- How can we (parents) help with homework?
- How much help should we (parents) give?
- What if we (parents) do not understand our child's assignment?
- How much time should our children spend each night on homework?
- Can our children do homework while listening to music or watching television?
- Do teachers really want us (parents) to ask them questions about homework?
- Our child seems bored by homework. Is this normal?
- What if our child still is not turning homework in?
- Should we reward our child for doing homework?

The book in hand helps answer these questions and many more that parents and others who care for children most often ask about homework at various levels of school education. It examines the efficacy of homework as an instructional method, develops a sequential model of the factors that influence homework outcomes and proposes homework policy and guidelines for teachers, schools, students and parents. Included are pragmatic ideas for helping students complete homework assignments successfully, for teachers to create and assign creative and challenging homework that may make the students *to think*.

In short, it has been tried to traverse the whole terrain of homework education. Without presuming to be encyclopedic, an attempt has been made to take cognizance of the predominant elements, concepts and assumptions that have characterized homework as an intellectual discipline.

This book is a synergetic product of many minds and here I would like to render a note of thanks to all those who have helped me directly or indirectly in completion of this book. I express my deep and sincere gratitude to those profound and prolific writers whose ideas have inspired me. Dr. Harris Cooper deserves a special mention whose ideas have influenced me a lot. I am also inspired by the works of J.A. Butler, Canter and Hauser, Doyle and Barber, Sharp and Paulu, Zental and Goldstein, Sonna, Rich, P. Mortimer, E. Klavan and many others.

Apart from authors, there are many persons to whom I feel indebted for the inspiration and assistance necessary for this book that has seen the light of the day. First and foremost among them are my students who have not only participated in countless "learning to learn" classroom sessions which I love to call sessions of cognitive dances, but have also greatly contributed to my own potential to continue to learning. Among the students one name, which deserves a special mention, is Mr. Sanjeet, who has been instrumental in the culmination of the idea behind writing this book. I feel honoured and privileged to thank my Founder President, Rao Birender Singh Ji, Ex-union-minister, Govt. of India, for his encouragement and moral support. He is the one who always motivates and inspires people for scholarly deeds. My principal Shri H.S. Yadav and faculty colleagues have provided support, advice and encouragement in this ongoing process as well.

I feel privileged to express my heartfelt thanks to Prof. R.P. Sharma and Prof. Girishwar Misra who have been generous in giving all help and guidance from time to time. Their timely and prudent interventions have indeed helped me immensely in navigating to safer waters. I am also thankful to Shri A.K. Nagar and Dr. Ashok Kumar for their support and encouragement. I will always remain grateful to Mr. S. Dureja and Mrs. Preeti Kiran Dureja whose loving and caring affection will keep on motivating me to do more constructive and creative work throughout my life.

More concretely, my family and my wife, Mrs. Sangeeta Sharma has been a continual source of encouragement and insight over the last three years. My wife and I had many long and fruitful conversations in conjunction with her reading and editing this manuscript. Such a companion is a great and rare gift. It will be hard and impossible to forget sweet, encouraging and inspiring sentence, "papa, kam kal lo" uttered by my little son Advait who is just two years old. My father-in-law Shri Shyamlal Sharma has become a source of inspiration for me who is retired but not tired at all. I am grateful to my parents and brothers whose love, affection, support and encouragement helped me to accomplish all the valuable tasks in my life, including the present work.

Last but not least, I am thankful to Atlantic Publishers & Distributors for giving this book its present shape.

Arbind Kumar Jha

CONTENTS

INTRODUCTION: PURPOSE AND PERSPECTIVE

1

It is universally admitted that knowledge and skills are the highest common denominators of all human achievements recognized in the form of art, civilization, culture, literature, philosophy, science, law, education etc. The last mentioned pursuit, education, is beyond any doubt or controversy the greatest beneficiary of knowledge. It not only assimilates this funded capital of humanity, transmitted down the ages, it also preserves and reproduces it in its new form and contextual contours. This functional duality of education concerning knowledge and skills invites many disciplinary safeguards to retain the sanctity of knowledge and skills in its 'essence' and 'expression', as homework education, serves as the ready reckoner for any eventuality that teachers may experience in their course of its march towards teaching-learning and realization of its avowed goals and objectives. Homework education with all its strength and limitation, proclaims a tool in hand that not only meets the pragmatic needs of education, but also extends the operational boundaries of teaching and learning to register qualitative advance on run-of-the-mill function of education at different levels.

Formal education system is one of the many modes that have been devised by every civilized world considering it as one of the many potential means to socialize and educate human beings. Today, every human being, across the class or cultural barrier, recognizes the immense importance attached to education. Due to its importance and prominence, a conscious and deliberate attempt has been made to formalise education. Consequently formal education is growing by leaps and bounds in every nook and corner of the world to impart education in a systematic and organized way. This formal education is involved with both the world of ideas and the world of practical activity as good ideas can lead to good practices and good practices can lead to good ideas. Also education is both a product and a process. As a product, education is what we receive through learning — the knowledge, ideals and techniques that we are taught. As a process, it involves the act of learning itself; in this case education becomes synonymous with the act of educating someone or being educated oneself.

To provide formal education, schools have been established all over the world. Why schools? It is the educational task of a society to preserve, transmit and improve three kinds of subject matter: what is useful or necessary in satisfying physical wants — to wit, vocational skills; what permits harmonious living — customs, rules, manners and what explains or predicts natural events — theories or ceremonies by which man seeks to control his present and future life. To achieve these educational goals, schools have been established with certain characteristics. Primarily, the school is an agency charged with the specialized task of simplifying the learning environment. It is a place where pupils can intensively pursue a restricted number of studies without the distraction of too many competing demands and where they can abstract ideas or theories of nature with which to interpret complex events of life. The school can economically arrange the conditions necessary to the learning of difficult ideas — ideas requiring ordered and prerequisite experiences and the deliberate noting of cause-and-effect relationships. By placing a child in artificial and selective situations, which are likely to give rise to understanding that would not occur by chance or would not be extended in a systematic fashion, the schools render a unique service. It is the business of the school to see that the child must grow. The ability to read and to apply principles, postulates, theorems and other abstractions to new situations develops only when the situations, by prearrangements, lead to generalizations and offer practice in applying the content to new events.

Second, a school is characterized by its chief resource, the teaching staff. As professional educators, teachers are prepared to share specific processes and notions drawn from the various disciplines — humanities, sciences, etc. Teachers' influence over his students is immeasurable. People send their children to them at a time when their minds and hearts are most receptive to new knowledge and new learning. The values of their parents or their social class have not yet hardened around them. Thus, teachers' ideal is to try hard to draw out the best in each of these young pupils considering teaching as rewarding profession. But, teaching also commands its price. To transmit knowledge, to make it clear, to relate it to the interests and capacities of all students — these functions require consummate power and skill. Assigning homework is one of the many skills, which are used by teachers to extend and reinforce learning, which ultimately help the child to transform the learnt information into knowledge.

Third, because all children are required to attend the school, it is uniquely fitted to the job of supplementing the values of a primary group by making clear the premises of the larger social order. The child's limited views derived from informal resources must be amplified by broader interpretations if society is to have both unity and diversity.

Last but not the least, as an agency of formal education, the schools are expected to grant access to facts and ideas that lie behind rational judgements in human relations. But, in making clear the considerations on which connoisseurs base their evaluations in these areas, care must be taken that the school itself exemplify the best of human relations and aesthetics to which this knowledge is expected to apply.

Every school of world has got some form of curriculum to impart knowledge and life skills to students. The curriculum consists of the means of instruction used by the school to provide opportunities for student learning experiences leading to desired learning outcomes. In most present day discussion and writing, these means of instruction include the classroom studies, the guidance or counselling programme, school and community service projects, school related work experience, the school library and those activities known as co-curricular activities. Thus, we can say that curriculum provides a broader framework to the teacher regarding what to teach and how to teach to students to make them learn. This way teaching and learning are the central activities of the curriculum planning, development and its transaction.

Now, what is teaching? To answer this question today we have a complete discipline called 'Pedagogy' to bank upon. Apart from rendering help in clearing conceptual cobwebs, homework education can provide guided lives for pedagogy, which can bring about substantial change in the art and science of teaching. Pedagogy is defined as 'any conscious activity' designed by one person to enhance learning in another. It encompasses not only teaching, but learning as well. However with the advancement of education, there is sea change in the roles and function of the teacher, *vis-a-vis* classroom transactions. The *laissez faire* approach, the interactive sessions, the dialogical and participatory forums of teaching and above all the 'child centred' education have all made it obligatory for the teachers, curriculum planners, policy-makers and educationists to recast their teaching-learning strategies into the new progressive mould, while 'received wisdom' reigned supreme in the field of pedagogy in the past, the newer nuances today would require greater initiative to be passed on to the child to come up. Learning on the part of the student is more important than teaching. It is not enough to put the learner in possession of truth; it is far more essential to put him/her on way to discover the truth.

The traditional definition of pedagogy is that it is a science of teaching. Modern understanding regarding pedagogy is: "any conscious activity by one person designed to enhance learning in another". This is clear from the above two understandings that pedagogy is not confined to teaching only but, it encompasses learning, too as to teach is to try deliberately to promote certain learnings. Jerry H. Gill (1995) has emphatically said, "Teaching is primarily a form of learning, a way of continuing to participate in the dance of cognitive activity and helping others learn to do so at the same time."

Recently, researchers into pedagogy not only endeavour to investigate how teachers organize subject-matter in their own minds, but are also interested in the teacher's ability to understand and apply the subject matter in different ways, according to the context of their classes, the sequence of lessons, and their knowledge of the learning groups and individuals. Conclusively we can say that teacher's job is not only to teach but also to make their learners to learn.

Let us discuss what is teaching. Teachers' conceptions of teaching have more recently been elicited. Samuelowicz and Bain (1992) have located these conceptions on an ordered continuum:

1. Imparting information.
2. Transmitting knowledge.
3. Facilitating understanding.
4. Changing students' conceptions.
5. Supporting student learning.

These conceptions represent different profiles on five dimensions: the learning outcome, the view of knowledge, the role of student's knowledge, the degree of reciprocation and the control of content.

Teachers' conceptions of teaching are an important focus. Also, the central question in understanding pedagogy might be: 'How do teachers' views of learning relate to their views of teaching?' There are five broad categories of what people generally assume 'learning' to mean:

- Getting more knowledge.
- Memorizing and reproducing.
- Acquiring and applying procedures.
- Making sense or meaning.
- Personal change.

What is the relation between teachers' conceptions of teaching and their conceptions of learning? Trigwell and Prosser (1996) offer two interesting findings. First, those teachers who saw a strong connection between teaching and learning were those who viewed teaching as mainly transmitting the syllabus and learning as accumulating knowledge in order to satisfy external demands. Second, those teachers with more sophisticated conceptions saw teaching and learning as different but inextricably linked processes. Although such teachers held more sophisticated conceptions of learning, they sometimes adopted lower level approaches to teaching — whereas the teachers with simpler conceptions of learning rarely adopted higher-level approaches.

Both these findings can be interpreted as teachers' simplifying the relationship between teaching and learning. In first case, many teachers adopt lower-order views of teaching in response to, for instance, examination pressures and organizational constraints. They simplify the goals in order to cope with the demands. In the second case, teachers simplify practice in order to cope with the complexity of the classroom. Teachers are aware of this tendency to simplification for, although some describe their ideal as using pupil-centred methods, they cite the everyday constrains of the classroom as being the reasons for their actual choice of methods (Chandra, 1987).

There may be the difference of perception in viewing the relationship between the teaching and learning and accordingly they may be adopting the approaches. Also, teachers use different method to impart contents of the curriculum, but, there is no doubt that they all use the same method or technique to reinforce and extend the learning i.e. assigning homework. The question of homework education brings in its train a host of other contentious issues. What is homework?, what are types of homework?, how homework is designed and assigned?, what are homework resources?, how do we judge the efficacy of homework assignment? etc. — these are question which have evoked multiple response from the people concerned. These are the problems, which need to be studied in terms of aspects that are theoretical as well as practical in nature. Therefore, this is an attempt to revisit Homework Education to see its import and implications for modern education.

Homework is the prime window into the school for the parents to see, understand and connect with the academic mission of the teachers. It is the primary area in which children, parents and schools interact on a daily basis. Yet it gets less systematic thought and attention than any other key component of education. Other than the admonition that kids should do more of it, we pay almost no attention to how to improve its design and content, its methods and practices. Nor do we do much to prepare teachers to use and evaluate homework, to hold administrators accountable for monitoring the homework load or to cultivate parent's collaboration. Homework remains an orphan child of the educational excellence movement.

The debate over homework must be redirected. To increase students' buy-in it is time to rethink how to make homework a more valued part of the pedagogic process. In addition to promoting academic achievement, homework can inculcate habits of self-discipline and independent study and can help inform parents about the educational agenda of their school. We must find ways to make homework an interesting and challenging educational experience for students, instead of the uniform, seat-bound, memorization focused solo exercise it has been. Otherwise, all our talk about high standards and improving student achievement will run up against the same roadblock that has stymied the pursuit of educational excellence in the past.

Keeping in view the urgent needs of making homework an intellectual discipline, a sincere attempt has been made to develop this book in hand to answer to questions like — what is homework?, what is its purpose?, what method and criteria should be adopted while assigning homework to different age group pupils?, how to involve parents in the process of completion to homework assignments?, how to develop guidelines regarding homework policy?, how to make responsible for completing homework? and many more such questions.

The book is an endeavour to make and establish homework as an intellectual discipline. A sincere attempt has been made to convince all the stakeholders of education that homework is one of the most powerful tools of learning experience. The method of this book is to present basic theoretical understanding and methodological ideas about homework assignment, which are essential to the investigation and solution of homework problems faced by students, teachers and parents. A second and more important reason for the method of the book is that at the very outset it provides some necessary ideas for critical assessing information that comes directly out of purpose of assigning, completing and evaluating homework. Stemming from the emphasis upon a sound practical and theoretical basis as the perquisite for solutions to practical problems, this book has been organized in such a way as to present relevant conceptual understanding of homework as before discussing some problems and its solution faced on the part of students and parents. In short, the style is interactive cum suggestive.

Chapter-2 highlights the need and importance of homework along with citing substantial research findings. In this chapter the author has mentioned the hidden values of homework as an effective learning tool. Along with need and importance, constructive purposes of homework in the context of child's educational experience have been depicted to a great extent. Here, the reader will find how homework helps to develop positive aspect of parents' relationship with the children. Last but not the least, why homework assignments should not be used as punishment.

Chapter-3 outlines the types and nature of homework. First of all, an attempt has been made to define homework from diverse perceptual understanding. Homework from different perspective — such as parents, students, teachers and schools etc. — has been discussed in detail. From the perspective of reinforcement theory of leaning, it has been shown how homework can be viewed as a powerful tool to extend learning. Also, it is an effective tool not only for promoting leaning but also fostering retention. Homework takes many forms and to be effective needs to be imaginative and creative and consequently it will put tremendous responsibility in the learner and above all it will give students an extended opportunity to learn in a meaningful way. In this chapter various types of homework have been discussed in detail. Special emphasis has been given on Co-operative type homework. Why teachers should try to make homework a cooperative homework instead of solitary activity — has been explained logically as co-operative homework assignments provide wonderful opportunity to students to learn and develop many necessary social skills to work cooperatively.

Chapter–4 spotlights some of the contentious issues which evoke response from parents, teachers, students, educationists and all those who value and practice homework and its import for various disciplines or pursuits of life. Many practical concerns on the part of various stakeholders have been discussed in such a manner, as these appear ours only. Under homework and parents section, practical measures have been suggested for the question like How can I help my child with his or her homework?, What strategies parents should adopt while tackling homework?, How to monitor assignments?, What parents should know about homework assignments?, What to do when the child doesn't understand the homework?, How to adapt homework assignments to maximize child's strength?, How to share concerns with the teacher?, How much help with homework is appropriate?, What precautional measures should be adopted while helping the child to complete homework assignments?, How to help children struggling to manage difficult or long-term assignments?, How to help child make a dull or boring homework task more enjoyable?, What to do when the child takes too long to complete homework?, What to do when our child rushes through homework and makes careless errors?, etc. Parental involvement and responsibilities have also been described in detail.

Under homework and teachers section some practical measures have been suggested to teachers while developing and assigning homework assignments. Practical measures are to see that the teacher should make sure students see the relevance of homework; justification of assignments; show respect for students; assign homework regularly and consistently; make sure students understand the purpose; make assignment focused and clear; make homework varied; create assignments that challenge students to think and to integrate; give homework that makes learning personal; involve and communicate with parents and many more.

Under the section of homework and students, subtle suggestions are there to help the students to make most out of their homework assignments. It has been discussed that what their personal responsibilities are; what strategies they should adopt for making up missed homework etc. Why is it necessary for the students to comply with teacher's guideline regarding homework?

In Chapter-5, the role of research in improving homework practices has been highlighted. Also, it has been established how the research outcome has helped the stakeholders of education to develop and implement homework policies and practices in the schools to help students to achieve better achievements and goals in education and life. Different researches conducted in the area of homework policies and practices have been described to assist teachers, parents and students for better performance. Some researchers have urged the schools to take a fresh look at homework and its potential for engaging students and improving student performance. The key, they say, is to take into account grade-specific and developmental factors when determining the amount and kind of homework. So, what is appropriate? What benefits can be expected? What makes for good homework policies? Research findings have provided a sound theoretical insights and pragmatic ideas to be implemented effectively to establish homework education as an intellectual discipline.

In this chapter, some suggestions have been given regarding what kind of further researches are required which may be helpful for the potential researchers who are going to conduct research in the field of homework. For example, in addition to studying homework's overall effectiveness, researchers should examine how variation in assignments might influence their efficacy. One obvious question is whether homework is more effective for some subjects than for others. Some researches should be conducted related to differences in homework assignments. For example, there may be considerable evidence that homework results in better achievement if material is distributed across several assignments rather than concentrated only on material covered in class that day. Homework that requires students to practice material already taught, as well as assignments meant to prepare students for upcoming lessons, both may prove beneficial. Some researches should be conducted in which researchers compare a homework feedback strategy (e.g., grading, instruction, or evaluative comments) with a no-feedback approach. Some studies focusing on the impact of the homework environment and form of task in relation to individual learning styles need to be conducted. Many other useful topics also find a place.

Chapter-6 depicts need and importance of providing respectful place in Teacher Education programme at various levels such as J.B.T./D.Ed., B.Ed., M.Ed. and the level of Research courses i.e. M.Phil. and Ph.D. In this chapter some questions have been raised why in Teacher Education programme, some thing like Homework Skill has not been introduced on the pattern of various skills in teaching under micro-teaching programme which is conducted before pupil-teachers visit the schools for teaching practice. Some practical measures have been suggested regarding introducing and establishing Homework as an intellectual discipline in Teacher Education programmes at various levels.

In chapter-7, general strategies have been highlighted keeping in view the different needs of different producers and consumers of education.

In the last chapter, which is entitled as "Some Contentions", a summary of the key points of the book has been arranged in a coherent manner to arouse further curiosity in the minds of teachers, parents, students and policy-makers which is going to prove beneficial for the entire educational world in the time to come.

In short, the writer has tried to traverse the whole terrain of homework education. Without presuming to be encyclopedic or thesaurus, an attempt has been made to take cognizance of the predominant elements, concepts and assumptions that have characterized homework as a discipline. The specific features of various facets of homework policy and practices have been underlined.

WHY HOMEWORK? 2

2.1 NEED AND IMPORTANCE OF HOMEWORK

What homework can do? What is the importance of homework? How does it correlate to every day life and its affairs and to lessons? Every body would agree that as a learning tool, there is every need to make it effective and for this we must understand certain important points like — need and importance; objectives or purposes; various factors; advantages and disadvantages etc.

Need and Importance

Homework is one aspect of the general education that has been widely recognised as an important tool of success. Teachers have used homework, since time immemorial, to provide additional learning time, strengthen study and organizational skills and in some respect, keep parents informed of their child's progress. Homework can help children develop good habits and etiquettes. It can teach children self-discipline and sense of responsibility. More importantly, it can encourage a love of learning.

From the perspective of classroom teaching and learning, homework enables children to cover topics taught more thoroughly and with greater speed and accuracy and so that the activity of self-study becomes a natural complement of teaching. It helps both teacher and pupils to see if what has been taught have been understood fully or not. In a way it creates a dialogue between teachers and students. A teacher can examine the pupils' work in depth to find out their strength and weaknesses and make comments and give guidance to correct and help them.

It is found that some students are very good at acquiring information but poor in its application. Homework checking by the teachers can provide an opportunity to both the teachers and the students to identify, which area is stronger or which area is weaker among the major components of cognitive domain such as knowledge, understanding, application and skill.

Children become more disciplined when studying on their own and can develop confidence in them, which may help them in future studies in higher education where the emphasis on progress is through self-development.

Becoming motivated and developing a discipline to do homework is as important as school education because education is not a progress that is undertaken only in school hours. It is a life long activity where one is continually striving to improve oneself and here habit of completing homework can be a big handy.

The importance of homework in view of self-study cannot be overestimated whether the teacher sets it or planned by the students. It may be possible for students to pass examinations without attending classes if given guidance but few of them could pass examinations without homework and study undertaken in the home.

Homework is a great predictor of success at any level of education — primary, secondary, senior secondary etc. If students want to achieve good percentage of marks or grades, it is important for the students to have higher competition rate on homework. The more homework students complete, especially from class six to twelve, the better they do in school according to research conducted by psychologists Harris Cooper, James J. Lindsay and Scott Greathouse (1998) of the University of Missouri — Columbia and psychologist Barbara Nye, of Tennessee State University.

It is the job of teachers, parents, administrators and especially children to make homework work. Schools cannot singularly teach all of the attitudes and enable the child to acquire all the knowledge and skills necessary for a fulfilling life. Let us discuss need and importance of homework from the perspective of various agents of education.

Teachers assign homework for a variety of reasons: to help students review, practice, apply and integrate what has been learnt in the class; to help them prepare for the next class session or get ready for the next day's class; to extend student exploration of topics more fully than class time permits; or to help students gain skills in self-directed learning and using resources such as libraries, reference materials and encyclopedias.

Homework is important for the students as it can develop good habits and attitudes. It can also help students to work independently, encourage self-discipline and personal responsibility. Homework assignments provide some youngsters with their first chance to manage time and meet deadlines. Above all it encourages a love of learning. Through homework students develop mastery by practicing what they have learnt in a limited time period in the class. Quality like fundamentals of working independently may be developed through homework assignment in a systematic and organized way. Also, through homework students can develop research skills such as locating, organizing and condensing information in a meaningful and purposive way.

Homework assignments can have many benefits for students, which they can use in their adult life. Homework can help students develop study skills that will be of value even after they leave school. It can teach them that learning takes place anywhere, not just inside the classroom. Homework can benefit children in more general ways as well. An organized homework programme helps students to gain the appropriate skills and staying power that will assist them to pole vault the challenges faced by the students during the schooling period. Also, it can foster many positive character traits, which are helpful in leading life successfully in various areas. It provides an opportunity for development of self-confidence and self-motivation — the vital components of one's personality.

Now, from the above descriptions of importance of homework, it can be asserted that the potential benefits of homework are indisputable. With the right focus, the work students do at home can reinforce and strengthen the learning and they can also learn how to transform the learning from short-term to long-term. There is a significant correlation between the assigning the homework by the teachers and completing it by the students. Student achievement rises very significantly when teachers regularly assign the home assignments and students' completion of it.

Home assignments provide students unique experience if following directions, making right judgements and comparisons, raising additional questions for study. It provides with opportunity to apply learning and experience necessary practice. It can be used as an effective tool to make students aware and self-responsible for their personal achievements.

Students may not always view homework as a pleasant experience, but if the assignments serve a good purpose and parents reinforce the completion of the tasks, students will benefit by gaining higher grades or marks, better study habits and a more positive attitude toward school and learning.

Homework can bring parents and teachers closer together; parents who supervise homework and assist their children with assignments learn more about their children's education and about the school (Paulu, 1995). Some educationists call homework an intersection between home and school. Some call it a bridge that joins schools and parents. Peg Sands (1999) identifies homework as Home links because it is the link between home and school. Through home links, parents have an opportunity to reinforce learning to become involved meaningfully in their child's holistic learning and education. From the school's perspective there is the opportunity to monitor students' independent progress. For parents, homework is a window through which they can observe their children's educational progress and express their positive attitude towards children's learning and their school. As children grow older, homework and the amount of time engaged in homework, increases in importance.

Work at home is a valuable and essential part of schoolwork and can help raise standards of achievement. At home, it is the duty of the parents to see and monitor the progress of homework. Here, it will not be an exaggerated fact to say that homework is the prime channel through which the parents connect with the academic mission of the teachers. It is the prime area in which children, parents and schools interact on a daily basis. Yet it gets less systematic thought and attention than any other key component of education. Other than the admonition that kids should do more of it, we pay almost no attention to how to improve its design and content. Nor do we do much to prepare teachers to use and evaluate homework, to hold administrators accountable for monitoring the homework load or to cultivate parents' collaboration. Homework remains an orphan child of the educational excellence movement. Parents need to take a lead in this direction otherwise, homework...the mere word can stir immediate negative feelings. It can be the source of battles, frustration and even tears. Homework doesn't have to be the ultimate monster and it does have definite benefits for children. We must keep in mind that the homework is our child's responsibility. Day-to-day experience as well as research has shown a strong correlation between homework and student achievement and the development of critical skill.

Homework is intended to be a positive experience that encourages children to learn and also assignments should not be viewed as punishment. According to Paulu (1995), children who spend more time on homework, on average, do better academically than children who don't and the academic benefits of homework increase in the upper grades. Research on homework regarding relationship between homework and student achievement has greatly strengthened the case for assigning homework. "Studies generally have found homework assignments to be most helpful if they are carefully planned by the teachers and have direct meaning to students" (Paulu, 1995).

Homework assignments give parents insight into the school curriculum and offer a greater opportunity for student learning to occur. Parents must realize that homework not only creates a commitment for children to undertake tasks that will further their academic development but also a commitment by the school to maintain better supervision on children's progress.

Further, listening to a teacher in class is the passive way of learning. Once children have been taught a topic they must spend time on their own reading about it and undertaking exercises at their own pace to ensure that they understand what they have been taught. Homework enables children to cover topics taught more thoroughly and with greater speed and so the activity of self-study becomes a natural complement of teaching.

Parents must realize that homework helps both teacher and pupils to see if what has been taught have been understood. In a way it creates a dialogue between them. The homework shows the teacher if pupils have fully understood what is being taught. The teacher can examine pupils' work in depth to find their strengths and weaknesses and make comments and give guidance to correct and help them. Further, the parents must realize that homework is very important as children become more disciplined when studying on their own and can develop confidence in themselves to encourage them to undertake future studies in higher education where the emphases on progress is through self-development.

Although we often do not consider that homework serves a school administrative role, it offers schools an opportunity to let parents know what their children are learning. Thus, homework can play a public relations role by keeping parents informed about class activities and policies. Homework can also fulfil an administrative role in helping schools achieve their, overall mission of improving student's achievement.

Homework is a bridge that joins schools and parents. From the school's perspective there is the opportunity to monitor student's independent progress. The homework not only creates a commitment for children to undertake tasks that will further their academic development but also a commitment by the school to maintain better supervision on children's progress. Review of homework policy can provide an opportunity to schools and its administrators to reformulate curricular contents and intents, which may suit the demands of the society and needs and inspirations of the people.

From the learning perspective too, homework is very important, as it is a powerful way to extend learning. Well-planned formulated, appropriate and purposeful homework can reinforce, maintain and extend classroom learning. It can stimulate new learning. It can increase the involvement of each student with the learning task. It can be one of the best tools to establish a unique relation between parents and child, home and school on the importance of learning. Well-integrated homework can promote creative learning insight.

Homework is valuable for the following reasons too:

- It allows children of all ages and at various stages of school life to develop the practice of working on their own without pressure from the teachers or other children.
- It helps reinforce basic skills learnt during the school days and thereby aid progress.
- Work at home can provide the quiet and private conditions needed for creative and thoughtful work of all kinds.
- It allows pupils to use materials and other sources of information that are not always available in the classroom.
- It involves parents and others in the children's work for their mental benefit. Parents can gather information about the nature and standards of their children's work, progress and education.
- It provides appropriate opportunities for long-term research project work and course work.
- It gives pupils valuable experience of working to deadlines and facilitates staff with their marking schedule.
- It gives opportunities to subject teachers to differentiate work for children.

The seven hidden values of homework:

(a) *Responsibility*: Homework is the child's responsibility. When the parents get too involved they set the process on its head. The lessons get done, but the real lessons don't get learned.

(b) *Independence*: Since this is the first time someone other than a parent assigns frequent tasks to the child, homework breaks new ground. How this golden opportunity is handled will enhance the child's progress toward self-direction.

(c) *Perseverance*: There is no point to a child's doing homework, if every time the child gets frustrated and the parents step right in and make it better. It is all right to let the child struggle a little with a problem.

(d) *Time management*: Children need to be told when to finish homework, not when to start it. That way instead of learning to waste time, the child learns to manage it.

(e) *Initiative*: Like a muscle, the ability to be a self-starter strengthens with exercise. That's why it is essential that the child decides when it is time to begin each homework assignment.

(f) *Self-reliance*: Homework can affirm a child's feeling of competency.

(g) *Resourcefulness*: The ability to be inventive in the face of problems is the very stuff of being human. Homework provides a wonderful setting for the child to practice such cleverness.

Homework is very much capable to help children to develop some other qualities like persistence, diligence and the ability to delay gratification. Janine Bempechat, a professor in the Harvard Graduate School of Education, says that the assignment of homework "helps children to develop qualities that all teachers like to see in classroom, such as persistence, diligence and the ability to delay gratification.

Harris Cooper (1994) presents immediate and long-term effects of homework:

Immediate: Students retain information and understand material better. Critical thinking and concept formation are increased. Information processing is improved and the curriculum is enriched.

Long-term academic: Learning is encouraged during leisure time. Attitudes toward school are improved. Study habits and skills are better.

Long-term non-academic: Students have greater self-direction and self-discipline. Time management is easier for students. Students are more inquisitive and participate in more independent problem-solving. Self-responsibility is cultivated when a student completed and hands in an assignment, no matter how small.

Available research studies and research literature also highlight the need and importance of homework. Research has begun to focus on the relationship between home and student achievement and has greatly strengthened the case for homework. Although mixed findings about whether homework actually increases student's academic achievement, many teachers and parents agree that homework develops students' initiative and fulfils the expectations of students, parents and the public. Studies generally suggest that homework assignments to be most helpful if they are carefully planned by the teacher and direct meaning to students.

According to some researchers, two ways to increase students' opportunities to learn are to increase the amount of time that students have to learn and to expand the amount of content they receive. Homework assignments may foster both these goals. Reforms in education have called for increased homework and as a result, reports show that students are completing considerably more homework than they did a decade ago.

For the researchers in the field of education, the issue of homework has historically been of great concern. Most agree that the purpose of homework should be to further facilitate learning, promote the development of strong study and organizational skills and encourage students to become self-disciplined, independent learners. However, with the increase in non-academic commitments and pressures placed on students, researchers have begun to explore not only the advantages of homework, but also the associated disadvantages. As educators, it is our responsibility to be aware of the knowledge available regarding homework and to integrate the findings into our own curriculum and our own homework policies.

- Homework is significant component of our education system and thus, it needs to be individualized to meet the specific needs of the child.
- Homework of a generic nature given to the entire class, regardless of interests and ability, is merely a time-filler. A must more useful and for more meaningful homework would be to ask each child to work upon on area of special interest to themselves.
- Studies conclude that additional benefits to achievement also result from homework. It has been found that student achievement rises significantly when teachers regularly assign homework and students consciously do it.
- The studies have suggested that the homework assignments also teach students to be independent learners. Homework gives student experience in following directions, making judgements and comparisons, raising additional questions for study and developing self-responsibility and self-discipline.
- The research studies have suggested that well designed homework assignments relate directly to class work and extend student's learning beyond the classroom and that homework is most useful when teachers carefully prepare the assignment, thoroughly explain it and give prompt comments and criticism when work is completed.

- Recent research in effective teaching skills points to the enormous importance of "independent practice" of homework. In order for students to learn and retain knowledge and concepts, they must experience success at using the knowledge or concepts completely on their own.
- Independent practice in the form of homework facilitates learning and provides a "bridge" between one day's learning and the next.
- Research studies have confirmed that open communication between parents and teachers is critical and homework does provide an excellent opportunity for this.
- Research indicates the students who conscientiously do their homework do better academically. They learn to follow directions, to organize and to manage time. They also learn to work independently and to find and use resources (Kline, 1998).
- Most of the research shows that there is a positive relationship between time spent on homework and achievement at secondary level school.
- Several international studies suggest that the relationship between time on homework and academic achievement may be curvilinear: pupils' doing either very little or a great deal of homework tends to perform less well at school than those doing 'moderate' amounts (Sharp, 2001).

An important point, which must be kept in mind, is that correlations between time on homework and achievement should not be taken as evidence that more time on homework necessarily leads to better achievement. The highlighted point is this that homework should be given proper attention and due importance.

The amount of time that students are expected to spend on homework will depend upon the age, ability, home environment and co-curricular activities of students including family and cultural obligations. It is important that students of all ages should have opportunities for free time, leisure and physical activities outside of school apart from homework obligation.

- For senior secondary school, the more homework time, the higher the achievement (within reason). For secondary school, more homework did improve achievement. For elementary school, homework time has not been consistently related to higher achievement, however, it is important for other functions, such as fostering independent study habits and letting parents know how their children are doing. Time spent by the parents reading with their children and sharing other enjoyable learning experience was found to be linked to school performance.
- Teaching responsibility and time management are important and often used as reason for homework, but this learning can be done with simple tasks (Cooper, 1989, Butler, 1987 and Copple, 1992).
- The single most important thing that children can do to grow academically is to read (Copple, 1992, and Adelman, 1995). Thus, reading kind of homework has a great significance at least academically.
- Appropriate kinds and amounts of homework raise achievement levels for students above primary levels. Homework is most beneficial when it is:
  - (a) Relevant to learning objectives.
  - (b) Appropriate to students' ability and maturity levels.
  - (c) Collected and reviewed during class.
  - (d) Supported by parents.
  - (e) Assigned regularly.
  - (f) Well explained and motivated.
  - (g) Used as an occasion for giving feedback (Butler, 1987, Holmes & Cross, 1989, Hossler, Stage and Galaghes, Paschal, 1988, Weinstein and Walberg, 1984).

How much homework a student should take, it is impossible to give a definite answer. How wisely a student uses practice time in class, the pace of work and the level of difficulty are variables unique to each individual. What is generally true, homework is a life skill and it enhances learning and responsibility.

2.2 PURPOSE OF HOMEWORK

Every intent, content and methodology of a curriculum design has its own importance with definite and clear-cut purposes. Similarly, homework as a method of extended learning has got not one or two but many purposes. The general purpose of homework is to review class material and practice certain skills. As children complete their assignments, they become more invested in and responsible for their learning. Homework assignments place demands on children that help them develop mental skills. It demands that a child concentrates, follows directions, organizes materials, solves problems and works independently. Homework offers a way to show a growing sense of competence and independence. Additionally homework helps forge an alliance between school and home. For teachers and administrators, homework is a cost effective way to provide additional instruction in practice.

Let us discuss the six constructive purposes for homework in the context of child's educational experience. Through (i) practice and (ii) participation in learning tasks, homework can improve our children's achievement. Thus, it would be expected that if homework assignments were completed accurately, not only would the children's general knowledge and grades or marks improve but the children would also increase mastery of basic academic skills, such as reading, writing, spelling and numerical ability.

Behind assigning the homework there is definite purpose that it works as one of the wonderful tools, which bring a strong sense of responsibility. The children's ability to bring an assignment home, gather and organize necessary materials to complete the assignment, return the assignments and receive a grade or marks, strengthens their sense of responsibility. Time management skills are learned. There is also improved (iii) development of personal skills such as time management gained by completing homework. Further, when homework proceeds smoothly it can become (iv) a positive aspect of parents' relationship with the children.

Finally, although we often do not consider that homework serves a school administrative role, it offers schools an opportunity to let parents know what their children are learning at school. Thus, homework can lay a public relations role by (v) keeping parents informed about class activities and policies. Homework can also fulfil (vi) an administrative role in helping schools achieve their overall mission of improve students' achievement.

Homework is also assigned having the purpose that it is a bridge that joins schools and parents. From the school's perspective there is the opportunity to monitor students' independent progress. For parents, there is the potential to gain a greater appreciation of education and to express positive attitudes towards their children's achievement (Zentall and Goldstein, 1999). It is expected that all schools, in consultation with their communities, will review their existing school homework policy to ensure it is relevant to the needs of their students.

Some more purposes of homework:

- It is a valuable part of schooling.
- It allows for practicing, extending and consolidating work done in class.
- It provides training of students in planning and organizing time.
- It develops a range of skills in identifying and using information resources.
- It establishes habits of study, concentration and self-discipline, which will serve students for their lives.
- It strengthens home-school links.
- It teaches the student to accept responsibility for his or her own work.

- It reaffirms the role of parents and guardians as parents in education.

The purpose of Homework is to:

- Encourage children to develop the skills, confidence and motivation to study effectively on their own.
- Consolidate and reinforce the skills and understanding developed in school, especially in literacy and numeric.
- Extend school learning through additional reading, project work etc.
- Develop and retain the involvement of parents in their own children's learning.
- Keep parents informed about the work the children are doing at schools.
- Enable the children to use extra resources for learning at home — e.g., Computer, Internet, Library, Adult knowledge etc.
- Encourage children, as they get older to develop the confidence and self-discipline needed to study on their own.
- Consolidate and reinforce the skills developed in lessons, to extend scope of learning and thus, to raise standards.
- Develop student's initiative, confidence and motivate research and study skills.
- Help students become independent, autonomous, and motivated learner prepared for lifelong learning.

The purpose and amount of homework changes as children grow and get older. At key stage i.e. lower stage the key purpose is to develop a partnership with parents and to involve them actively in children's learning with a focus on literacy and numeric. As children get older, the main purpose of homework is to provide all children with the opportunity to develop independent learning skills.

There is need to have a clear-cut guidance:

- To provide specific guidelines on homework for teachers, parents and students.

- To help promote continuity and consistency with homework practices.
- To help promote and foster positive experiences about homework.
- To help new teachers/parents/students adjust to homework practices.
- To help increase the land of communication between home and school, especially as it relates to homework assignments.
- Homework is meant to be a positive experience and to encourage children to learn.
- *Assignment should not be used as punishment.*

Creating high quality assignments with a purpose can be time consuming. A secondary school social studies teacher explains: "For much of the homework I assign (students) know that the next day I will use it as the basis of a more meaningful whole. They know there is a purpose to what I'm assigning. They know the knowledge is crucial to the next day's activity. Thus, the homework requires a fair amount of planning and thought as to why I am giving it in the first place.

The two major purposes of homework are to extend student learning and to involve parents in their child's formal education. A student should be incorrect if he/she states, "the teacher didn't tell us how to do this..." when referring to homework. Prior to something becoming homework, direct instruction, guided practice and checking for understanding take place. Long-term homework tends to be projects. It also teaches children the importance and value of advance learning. We hope that students quickly learn that if they put off completing a project until the night before it is due, they may have a large quantity of work and quality of their learning or finished product will not be their best. The question we want children to take seriously and ask themselves is, "Is this good enough to put my name in it?" The goal is to install pride in workmanship and set high expectations for quality.

A perennial issue regarding homework is "how much help should I provide?" The answer is "it depends". It is appropriate to help children sufficiently for them to become independent. When children are given too much help, they become dependent upon assistance. They also do not learn as much, and don't develop a strong work ethic. The key word here is 'work'. Work and learning are not always fun, and not always easy. That is life. Excellence is not achieved easily, or given away. It is earned via work and practice. Parents should provide a designated location for homework free from as many distractions as possible, and having the materials and supplies needed for the works. When the above occurs, children receive appropriate support and assistance, and they are learning that education is important to their parents as well as their teachers.

Homework should be:

- Part of learning process.
- Developmentally appropriate.
- Clearly defined.
- Returned promptly with comments.
- Used to assess student understanding.
- Supported and valued by teachers, students and parents.

There is need to have feeling that the time used by students to complete homework assignments is sacred. There must always be a place in our home for homework. Children have to understand that their work — schoolwork — is important and they get that message when families make homework a priority. Also, there is need to create mission statement that benefits homework as "any activity where learning is extended after school." This is not necessarily work done at home, but any work outside the classroom that isn't teacher directed. The ultimate purpose of homework is to increase learning and student success and to foster the development of positive character traits of responsibility and self-discipline.

Synoptically the purposes of homework include:

- *Practice/Review*: To reinforce and/or master basic skill already presented in class.

- *Preparation*: To introduce material to be presented in future lessons.
- *Extension*: To provide students with opportunities to transfer specific skills or concepts to new situation.
- *Application*: To enable students to connect skills and concepts to novel circumstances.
- *Creativity*: To enable students to be creative by performing certain tasks.

WHAT IS HOMEWORK?

3

3.1 WHAT IS HOMEWORK?

Homework serves as an intellectual discipline that definitely establishes study habits, eases time constraints on the amount of curricular contents and intents that can be covered in class, and supplements and reinforces work done in school. In addition to all these, it fosters students' initiative, independence and sense of responsibility, and brings home and school closer together. It is an excellent way to teach students the importance of starting staying with and completing a task. It is also an opportunity to teach students to do the best work he or she can.

It is well-accepted fact that homework is an important part of our students' education at school. Thus, we must believe that homework is truly an extension of the classroom, providing every student with the opportunity for enhanced extended learning. Homework assigned by the teachers is generally related to the curriculum and thus, due consideration is given to the developmental needs of young growing students. Thus, for better learning the required material in each curriculum area, the practice of homework is widely practical as one of the vital means. Teachers assign the homework in almost all schools considering it as their one of the many assigned compulsory roles. But, the prime responsibility of homework belongs to the students themselves. The teachers, parents and administrators also play an important and integral role in successful homework experience. Thus, there is need to have active communication as an essential factor throughout the homework process. On the basis of this very fact, homework is truly called as home links because it is the link between home and school. Through this home links, parents have an opportunity to reinforce learning, to become involved in their child's education.

From teachers' perspective homework is assigned to help students understand and review the work that has been covered in class. To see whether students understand the lesson or not? Also, assigning homework is to help students learn how to find and use more information on a taught subject. We can say that it is nothing but an extension or elaboration of class work. Teachers perceive homework as the link between school and home that shows what students are studying.

Almost all the learning theories have shown that the very fundamental thing about learning is to be willing to learn and homework provides a very good opportunity to learn. From learning perspective, teachers assign homework to students mainly to extend learning time so that already learnt things can be reinforced. Thus from the perspective of reinforcement theory of learning, homework is a powerful way to extend learning. It is an effective tool not only for promoting learning but also fostering retention. Homework takes many forms and to be effective needs to be imaginative and creative and consequently it will put tremendous responsibility on the learner and above all it will give students an extended opportunity to learn in a meaningful way. It can provide students practice in persevering and accomplishing goals and help them learn "to take responsibility for keeping their minds active".

Teachers assign homework not for a reason or two but for a variety of reasons — to help students to review, to practise, to apply and integrate already learnt knowledge. But, prime reason is to review class material and practice skills. As students complete their assignments, they become more invested in and responsible for their learning. Homework places demands on children that help them develop mental skills. It demands that a student concentrates, follows directions, organizes materials, solves problems and works independently. Homework offers a way to show a growing sense of competence and independence.

Some definitions of homework are as under:

- Homework is defined as "any work or activities which students attempting outside lesson time" is seen as an essential part of students' learning at school. In other words homework is any planned educational activities to be completed by the student outside of the regular class.
- Homework is defined as "task assigned to students by school teachers that are meant to be carried out during non-school hours" (Cooper, 1989). Omitted in this definition are: (a) in-school guided study; (b) home study courses, and (c) co-curricular activities.
- Homework is defined as a cost-effective instructional technique. It can have positive effects on achievement and character development and can serve as a vital link between the school and family.
- Homework is defined as important component of child's school experiences. It affords the opportunity for practice and review, and helps the child become an independent learner, as essential skill in school and beyond.
- For teachers and administrators, homework is a cost effective way to provide additional instruction in practice.
- Homework is defined as out-of-class tasks assigned to students as an extension or elaboration of classroom work.
- Homework is the time students spend outside the classroom in assigned activities to practice, reinforce or apply newly acquired skills and knowledge and to learn necessary skill of independent study (Butler, 1987).
- Homework is a task initiated and/or motivated in the classroom related to the objective of the course studied which is normally completed during out-of-class time.
- Homework may take the form of additional practice on exercises, reading of material on a specified subject, in-depth follow-up of classroom activities, or independent project work related to the subject.

- Power, Karustis and Hobboushe (1997) define homework as "assignments given by teachers that are to be performed by students outside of or during non-instructional classroom time.
- Homework assignments are designed to reinforce classroom instruction, increase understanding and retention, transfer extended classroom instruction, prepare for class discussion and provide curriculum enriched opportunities.
- Through homework and out-of-class assignments, students have the opportunity to reinforce and/or extend academic and learning skills taught in the class. Homework also contributes to the students, development of such skills as working independently, organizing time, developing effective work habits, and developing self-discipline in accepting responsibilities.
- Homework for the school-age child is an opportunity to learn the valuable organizational skills for strong study habits.
- Homework enables children to cover topics taught more thoroughly and with greater speed and accuracy and so the activity of self-study becomes a natural complement of teaching.
- Homework is both an extension and a reinforcement of class work. It is not as effective when done as an isolated exercise. This piece of exercise must be an integral one.

Above mentioned definitions of homework should not be taken as limitative as these may depend on purpose and perspective of the concept of home assignments.

As far as students' perspective is concerned, homework is "all by myself", "back off" and "call it quits at a reasonable hour". Here, all by myself means homework is the student's responsibility and should be done in private. Back off implies that the parents need to resist helping children with homework. They should help only if the child asks for assistance after a legitimate, determined effort to solve it himself or herself. They should not steal a child's struggle. Help should be brief and encouraging. Call it quits at a reasonable hour implies that student should set a time limit (remember setting an ending time is more important than setting a beginning time). Set a consistent deadline, this deadline can be temporarily extended for special projects and major homework tasks.

In the end it is desirable to note that our clear-cut and strong sense of understanding of the concept of homework will certainly provide all of us — as a teacher, parent, student, administrator — a new paradigm of thinking and vision to make this practice of assigning homework assignments more meaningful and purposeful to help us to move ahead towards better performance in the field of education.

3.2 TYPES OF HOMEWORK

Homework is defined as out-of-class tasks assigned to students as an extension to classroom work. There are at least four important skills to practice when it comes to home preparation and extension. There are numerous types of homework assignments that can be effective in various situations. The available literature indicates that there are five types of homework such as — Practice (to reinforce skills); Preparation (to get ready for activities); Extension (long-term assignments based on what is happening in class); Application (to apply in new concrete as well as abstract situation) and Creative (to apply knowledge in a creative or imaginative manner) and Cooperative (to work and learn cooperatively).

Practice type Homework

This type of homework is meant to *reinforce learning* and help the student-master specific skills. In other words, such assignments are assigned to strengthen newly acquired skills. For instance, students who have just learnt a new method of solving a mathematical concept of problem should be given sample problems to complete on their own.

This type of home assignments provides the student with an opportunity to continue that that has been presented in the class. Also, it provides students with the opportunities to apply the learnt concept, or review, revise and reinforce recently acquired specific methods or skills including: (a) consolidation exercises e.g. mathematics, including memorisation of tables, definitions, formula etc.; (b) revising information about a current topic; (c) practicing for mastery e.g. spelling words; (d) practicing words or phrases learnt in a language; (e) reading for pleasure; (f) writing essay etc.

People say practice makes perfect, but, we must remember that not all practice but only perfect practice makes perfect. This type of homework must be assigned as well as completed keeping in mind that this provides an opportunity to have sound and perfect practice.

Preparatory type Homework

This type of home assignments introduces material that will be presented in future lessons. These assignments aim to help students learn new material better when it is covered in class. In other words such assignments help students get ready for activities that will take place in near future in the classroom activities. This type of homework is generally defined as assignment aimed at preparing students for next unit or lesson in that subject.

Preparatory type homework is introduced or assigned to provide opportunities for students to gain background information on a unit or lesson of study so that they are better informed and prepared as well as for future lesson including: background reading; reading e.g. English text for class discussion; researching topics for a class unit of work; collecting items e.g. geometrical shapes etc.

Extension type Homework

Extension type assignments are frequently long-term continuing parallel class work. Students must apply previous learning to complete these assignments include science fair projects; statistical projects; mathematical projects and term papers. Such type of homework assignments is intended to extend a previously learnt skill, body of knowledge or the thinking process. Also, the purpose of such assignments is encouraging students to pursue knowledge individually and imaginatively including: writing e.g. a book review; making or designing something e.g. an art work; investigations e.g. history, local news; information and retrieval skills e.g. using a home computer to find material on the internet; monitoring e.g. advertising in particular newspapers.

This kind of homework asks students to apply skills they already have to new situations. Extension kind of home assignments is integration kind of homework which requires the student to apply many different skills to a single task.

Application type Homework

This type of home assignments is assigned to enable students to connect skills and concepts to the new concrete as well as abstract situations. From the learning perspective too, this type of homework has got immense potential.

Creative type Homework

This type of home assignments provide students with the opportunity to apply previously learned knowledge in a creative or imaginative manner. As is the general practice students are asked to solve questions or problems, but, in such type of homework assignments students are asked to formulate problems or questions which will lead the student to be creative in his or her own way. Also, creative and imaginative tasks will not make the home assignments monotonous. If students are not assigned with creative homework (or homework which demands creativity on the parts of students) may in the long run avoid using deep-level cognitive processing strategies, such as trying different ways to solve a problem.

Cooperative type Homework

This type of home assignments provides students with the opportunity to work and learn cooperatively. Teachers should try to make homework a cooperative homework instead of solitary activity. Cooperative homework assignments provide wonderful opportunity to students to learn and develop many necessary social skills to work cooperatively.

While assigning this type of homework, teacher will have to be bit extra careful. It is felt that homework does not have to be a solitary activity. Thus, the teachers should set cooperative homework assignments or tasks whose completion requires two or more students to work together. However, they should check first that students have the necessary social skills to work cooperatively and teach these skills if necessary. Bear in mind that successful cooperative homework requires both joint goals and individual accountability.

The homework assignments most enjoyed by the students are those that are performance based and require them to team up with a class member who lives in their neighbourhood. Working together is a real fun and thus they make learning fun. Also, the two elements — the amount of homework completed and the accuracy of that homework — has a positive effect on achievement. Cooperative homework may be effective in increasing both of these.

Typology of homework should not be confined to above-mentioned types of homework only. There may be several other types based on purpose and perspective. As far as category of homework is concerned, there are two general categories of homework — short-term and long-term homework assignments. Both are more effective when they are extensions of classroom experiences, Short-term homework is generally due in a day or two and is typically practise, remediation, and/or extension of recent classroom learning objectives.

Let us discuss some other types of homework: There is no doubt that homework is an effective tool for promoting learning and fostering retention. It takes many forms and to be effective needs to be:

Drill type: In its simplest form, homework enables children to drill the skills so that learning is mastered and retained. Drill assignments may be generated by the teacher and returned to class. Examples include: mathematics worksheets; flash cards; vocabulary words; computer games; spelling assignments etc.

Daily home study type: The purpose of daily home study is to offer the opportunity for students to develop consistent study habits. The practice of basic skills provides a firm foundation for more complex tasks. Examples include: parent/child reading; half an hour of silent reading; mathematics facts; writing (diary, letters, journal etc.).

Nightly assignments type: This type is there just to review or practice the already learnt class work.

Review type: This type of homework is there for test or exams.

Research type: Such type of homework is there for specific research activities.

Reading and/or writing type: This type of homework is assigned to develop reading and/or writing.

Projects type: This type of assignments is based on pragmatic methods, which may provide direct first hand learning experiences. All the projects work comes under this type of homework assignments.

Our understanding of above mentioned types and categories of homework assignments would certainly help all of us stakeholders of education to create better insight regarding homework activities taking shape at various levels. Consequently we all — curriculum planners and executors, teachers, parents, students — can delve deep into the intellectual aspect of homework to make it more meaningful and purposeful.

3.3 ADVANTAGES AND DISADVANTAGES

The conscientious completion of homework has a positive impact on a student's success in school. Thus, the importance of homework in promoting academic excellence and self-discipline cannot be over-emphasized. Students who fail to complete their homework assignments quickly fall behind their peers academically and socially. This may place enormous psychological pressure on the student. Left uncorrected, the student may become frustrated and disinterested in class. This often results in academic failure and truancy.

The list of possible advantages and disadvantages of homework is long and often surprising. Among the suggested advantages of homework, the most obvious is that it will increase students' retention and understanding of the material it covers. Less directly, homework can improve students' study skills and attitudes toward school and teach students that learning takes place outside as well as inside of school. Homework has numerous potential non-academic payoffs as well; most of these involve promoting student independence and responsibility. Finally, homework can involve parents and the broader community in schooling, increasing their appreciation of education and allowing them to reinforce students' achievement.

Homework helps child do better in school when assignments are meaningful, are completed successfully, and are returned with constructive comments from the teacher. An assignment should have a specified purpose come with clear instructions, be fairly well matched to a student's abilities and designed to help develop a student's knowledge and skills.

The possible disadvantages of homework are perhaps more interesting. First, some educators note that any activity can remain only for a limited. It follows that if students are required to spend too much time on academic material, they eventually will become bored with it. Second, homework limits the time students can spend on leisure-time and community activities that can impart important lessons, both academic and non-academic. Third, parental involvement, however well-meant, often becomes parental interference. Parents can confuse children if the teaching methods they employ differ from those of teachers. Fourth, homework can lead to undesirable behaviours such as cheating, either through copying of assignments or receiving assistance with homework that involves more than tutoring. Finally, homework could exacerbate existing social inequalities. Students from lower socio-economic homes are likely to have more difficulty completing homework than their more well to do peers.

Poorer students are also more apt to work after school or may not have a quiet, well-lit place to do assignments.

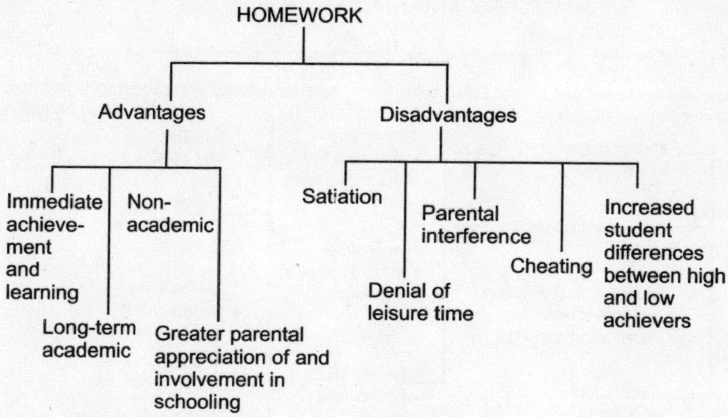

Advantages are:

(A) Immediate achievement and learning:

- Better retention of factual knowledge.
- Increased understanding.
- Better critical thinking, concept formation, information process.
- Curriculum enrichment.

(B) Long-term academic:

- Learning encouraged during leisure time.
- Improved attitude toward school.
- Better study habits and skills.

(C) Non-academic:

- Greater self-direction.
- Greater self-discipline.
- Better time organization.
- More inquisitiveness.
- More independent problem-solving.

(D) Greater parental appreciation of and involvement in schooling.

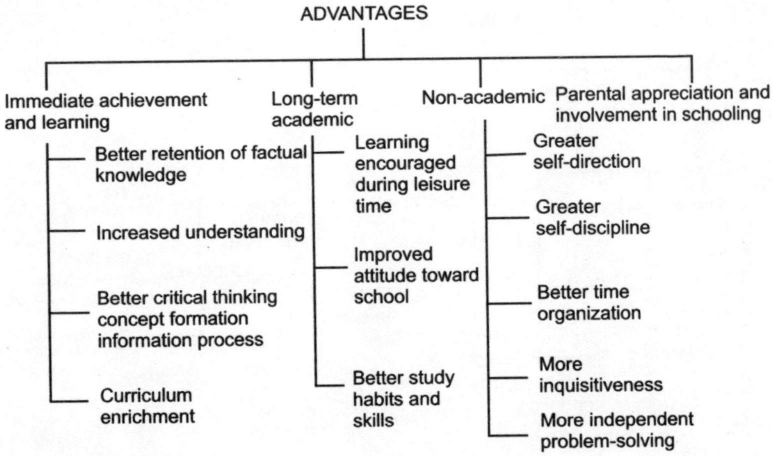

Disadvantages:

(A) Satiation:
- Loss of interest in academic material.
- Physical and emotional fatigue.

(B) Denial of access to leisure time and community activities:
- Parental interference.
- Pressure to compete and perform well.
- Confusion of instructional techniques.

(C) Cheating:
- Copying from other students.
- Help beyond tutoring.

(D) Increased differences between high and low achievers.

(E) Can cut into outside pursuits and cause pupils to develop ways to beat the system (copying etc.).

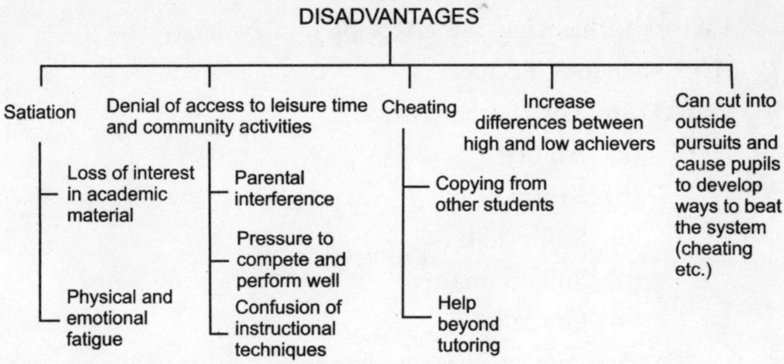

3.4 FACTORS AFFECTING HOMEWORK

There are numerous factors that affect the usefulness of homework. The factors are: student characteristics, the subject matter and especially grade level — that determine the benefits of homework.

Characteristics of the assignment are important as well. Homework assignments can be short or long, can have different purposes (such as the practice of old material, introduction of the new material, integration of skills, or extension of the curriculum), can be designed for individual students or whole classes, and can be completed by individuals or groups. The time and effort teachers take to develop assignments also varies.

When a student takes the assignment home, several factors will affect how it is completed including the student's other time commitments, the home environment and involvement of parents and others.

Finally, what the teacher does with assignments when students turn them in may affect homework's utility. Some teachers may simply collect assignments, whereas others go over them in class and provide written feedback, oral comments or grades: Other teachers may permit students to correct homework as art of the learning process and even provide extra credit toward grades.

Factors influencing the effect of homework:

1. Exogenous Factors:
   - (A) Student characteristics:
     - (a) Ability
     - (b) Motivation
     - (c) Study habits
     - (d) Subject matter
     - (e) Grade level
   - (B) Assignment characteristics:
     - (a) Amount
     - (b) Purpose
     - (c) Skills are utilized
     - (d) Degree of individualization
     - (e) Degree of student choice
     - (f) Completion deadlines
     - (g) Social context
   - (C) Initial classroom factors:
     - (a) Provision of materials
     - (b) Facilitators
     - (c) Suggested approaches
     - (d) Links to curriculum
     - (e) Other rationales
   - (D) Home-community factors,
     Competitors for student time,
     Home environments:
     - (a) Space
     - (b) Light
     - (c) Quietness
     - (d) Materials

Others involvement:
(a) Parents
(b) Siblings
(c) Other students

(E) Classroom follow-up
Feedback:
(a) Written comments
(b) Grading
(c) Incentives
(d) Testing of related content
(e) Use in class discussion

(F) Outcomes or effects:
(a) Assignment completion
(b) Assignment performance

3.5 HOMEWORK POLICY

What is good policy?

Experts advise schools to include teachers, parents and students in any effort to set homework policies. Policies should address the purposes of homework (not to be used as punishment); amount and frequency; school and teacher responsibilities (e.g., coordination of assignments, clear directions, home-school communications); student responsibilities; the role of parents or others who assist students with homework; and equity issues (accommodations for students with disabilities, availability of support and resources).

If the school does not already have a homework policy in place, it might discuss this with other teachers and administrators. Homework policies, which function to define a standard set of expectations for and beliefs about homework, can be shared and reviewed with students, parents, and teachers at the beginning of each school year. At minimum, homework policies should define the role of homework in learning at each grade level, and the specific responsibilities of teachers, parents, and students (Butler, 1987).

While some educators caution that school-wise policies for homework can become restrictive (Black, 1996), there are advantages to having a shared understanding of how homework is being used to support learning. Homework policies not only help define parents' role in homework, but also ensure that students and parents are informed about teachers' expectations. Another benefit of homework policies is that they allow teachers to develop a consistent, school-wise set of expectations for students, which is particularly helpful for students who have several different teachers throughout the day. Developing a homework policy is also a good way for educators to get together, review the research, and explore how homework can best be used to promote achievement and engagement in school.

Active parent involvement has been associated with numerous benefits for students, including increasing student motivation and engagement in school. When it comes to homework, though, parent involvement can take many different shapes, not all of which have a positive impact on learning. When working to increase student engagement and motivation, it is important to include parents and discuss ways they can support their children's learning both at school and at home (Patton, 1994; Paulu, 1998).

First, it is important that parents understand what role teachers expect them to play, especially in terms of homework (Gaillard, 1994; Paulu, 1998). What one-parent views as helping out, a teacher might perceive as interference or cheating. And what a teacher might take for granted that parents can do — such as signing off on homework or checking spelling words — a parent may not have the skills or the time to follow through on. Clearly, it is important to communicate with parents about how to best help children learn. It is also necessary for educators to be sure their expectations are realistic, given parents' skills and schedules (Paulu, 1998).

It is equally important to be clear with parents about what kinds of involvement are actually beneficial to students. Studies have shown that parents who offer rewards for grades, or who punish students for poor performance, may actually decrease students' motivation to do well (Dev, 1997; Patton, 1994). Fear of punishment, anxiety about meeting parents' expectations, and worrying about being compared to siblings not only cause stress for students, but can also detract from their intrinsic motivation and interest in learning (Dev, 1997). This is not to say that parents shouldn't be invested in how their children are doing in school. Rather, it suggests that there are more productive ways for them to be involved and show their interest in students' progress.

A good homework policy will go beyond the details of how homework is administered and focus on how assignments are designed. A lot of homework frustration arises when teachers "make do" with textbook exercises. Such assignments, week after week and year after year, contribute to the attitudes that homework is neither important nor beneficial for learning. Instead teachers should understand the different purposes of homework — from improving study skills to involving parents, and plan a productive mix of assignments to meet specific learning goals. The earlier we start teaching kids to become self-directed learners, the better. Homework is the first opportunity we have to do that.

For the homework policy to be implemented successfully, each group within the school community-members of the management, the administration, teachers, parents and students — must fulfil the following responsibilities:

In implementing a homework policy, the management and the administrations should:

- Establish and communicate the homework policy to teachers, students and parents.
- Periodically review the policy and evaluate its effectiveness.
- Monitor the implementation of the policy.

School Policy with respect to Homework: The policies and practices affecting students are those aspects of school's operation that organize students' experiences within the institution. For younger students, these policies and practices structure the parents' relationship with the school. In considering the school's policies and practices affecting students, educators should ask themselves such questions as "what is the school policy with respect to homework?"

The decisions that school makes regarding established policies and practices affect students enormously. Teacher's instructional decisions influence students feeling about (and success with) the curriculum, but the policies and practices in both classrooms and in the entire school proved the context for teacher-student interactions around instruction.

1. A safe and positive and constructive environment
2. A culture of hard work
3. A success orientation
4. A culture of respect and responsiveness to clients
5. Student leadership and decision-making
6. Minimal competition
7. A conducive culture for learning

   Educators should bear the following issues in mind when considering their schools cultures:

   (a) School cultures are slow to change.
   (b) Different spheres of student excellence merit recognition.
   (c) A school culture that supports student learning should be promoted within each classroom and in the school as a whole.

A safe and positive and constructive environment: Both the physical and psychological school environment must be safe for all students. Policies and practices must show respect for students, who should feel safe at school and feel that it is theirs. Consistency and predictability are a part of safety; rules and procedures must be fairly and consistently applied so that they are not regarded as capricious.

A culture of hard work: Students derive enormous satisfaction from tackling difficult tasks and succeeding on their own. If educators want students to experience the pride of success through hard work they will establish practices that reward hard work rather than natural endowment or luck. In addition, homework and grading/marking policies should not handicap students who don't "get it" on the first attempt; such students be given a second chance to succeed, and a third.

A success orientation: The goal of school policies and practices should be student mastery of the curriculum and development of their potential. There is no room in school truly committed to student learning for policies that are punitive, turn students away or undermine their confidence. If some students believe that they are forever relegated to a "low group" — that nothing they do will ever let them become leaders in student government, because they are somehow not regarded as part of the school's "elite" — they will turn their back on the benefits of school. If students regard challenging courses or membership in certain clubs as the province of only a select few, most will harbour no ambitions for each such opportunities.

A culture of respect and responsibilities: In many schools, particularly secondary schools, students feel that they are the least important people in building: they are kept waiting by teachers or the principal, they are summoned to the office for mysterious reasons and they feel that no one ever believes their side of the story. Taken together, the policies and practices in these schools do not produce an environment in which students feel respected as human beings and valued as full participants.

Student leadership and decision-making: Opportunities for student leadership can help define the culture of a school. These must not be restricted to an elite — these must be broad opportunities for students to develop leadership skills, such as by helping establish the homework guidelines, serving as lab assistants in science or leading a hand with younger students.

Decision-making relates more to how policies and procedures are derived than to what they are. Students of all ages value the opportunity to shape the rules by which they live. When they help create rules, students are more likely to understand the rationale behind them and will comply with them more willingly. In addition, the inclusion of student voices in the decision-making process provides educators with access to a valuable perspective. Rules and procedures are therefore likely to be stronger if students help create them than they would be if mandated by teachers and administrators alone.

Minimal competition: Despite knowing the corrosive efforts of competition, many educators continue, largely because of tradition, to create policies and practices that institutionalise competitiveness into the fabric of the school. Students should only compare against themselves in the classroom (e.g., by trying to "top" a previous assignment).

A conducive culture for learning: Learning is an active process, in which students must be engaged as genuine participants. And student learning is not limited to curriculum: students learn from homework and disciplined policies as well. Consequently, aspects of a school's policies that have an effect on student learning should be designed with active learning in mind: for example, if educators want students to assume responsibility for their behaviour, discipline policies should reflect a view of students as active decision-makers.

A school's culture for learning is the implicit sense among students regarding what is valued in the school and whether it is important to be a successful learner. In this context, the term "culture" is used in the anthropological sense, meaning the norms and values that prevail in a school setting. What is valued? Many schools suffer from a student culture in which it is not "tool" to be smart, work hard or earn high grades. Educators should bear the following issues in mind when considering their schools' cultures:

School cultures are slow to change: Some students, particularly those who have experienced little school success, build their reputations as class clowns. They project the image play the game. Even when faculty makes a concerned effort to change this student culture and support a success orientation, the students themselves may be resistant to change. As a result, high school teachers, particularly in required courses, may inherit students who have had a long history of failure and who are not prepared to risk their self-esteem and reputation with friends for the elusive goals of school success. A shift in school culture will take time.

Different spheres of student excellence merit recognition: Most secondary schools proudly display their athletic trophies and student athletes are publically recognized through school assemblies and the student newspaper. *Likewise, students with leads in the homework may be acknowledged.*

A school culture that supports learning should be promoted both within each classroom and in the school as a whole: This culture should be promoted in classrooms — where student creativity and commitment should be recognized on a daily basis as well as throughout the schools (e.g., through displays of student work, honour rolls, recognition assemblies or weekly lunches with the principal).

Teachers assign homework to students mainly to extend learning time. Students are in school for six hours or so each day; if they complete assignments at home, they can be actively engaged in learning for considerably longer than that.

A school's approach to homework depends on the age of the students. Although it is unreasonable to expect young children to spend long hours doing assignments, a well conceived homework policy helps students assume more responsibility for their own learning and allows students to continue learning beyond the school day.

As educators determine their school's approach to homework the following guidelines may be helpful:

- *Homework is important*: If assigned, homework must be completed; it should not be optional, but rather integral to the instructional programme. A school's homework policy should convey the importance the school attaches to homework and emphasize student commitment and responsibility for completing it.
- *Student must be able to complete assignments independently*: As a general rule, students should be able

to complete assignments without adult assistance at home. The reason for this is simple equity. Some parents are able to substantially assist their children by virtue of their own education: they can explain how to factor polynomials, for example or provide feedback on writing. But, this type of help, only some students will have the benefit of what amounts to a private tutor at home. It is essential that success in school not depend on the availability of parental assistance.

- *Assignments should be appropriate to completion at home*: Some assignments are inappropriate for homework — such as those that represent new learning or learning that requires frequent explanations or intervention by a teacher. More suitable homework assignments are those that ask students to practice previously learned skills, write essays or memorize vocabulary. Practice increases fluency and facility and repetition can enhance student mastery of a concept.
- *Links between home and school should be pursued*: Some assignments can integrate the home into the learning experience. After studying the Great Depression, for example eleventh standard history students and neighbours regarding their experiences during the Depression and its aftermath. Or third graders, after having learned to make bar graphs, can collect data regarding the different types of furniture in their homes and display the information in a bar chart; the next day the classroom wall will be covered with charts of chairs tables, beds and television from which patterns may be observed and hypotheses generated.
- *Educators should help students deal with emergencies*: When unforeseen events occur, students should not be unduly penalized. Some students, however, exhibit a pattern of suspicious "emergencies" — dogs after all can eat only so much paper. Teachers may need to help such students to develop a "plan B" that they can implement when emergencies arise.

- *Teachers should distinguish between completion and effort*: Students sometimes get stuck in the course of doing their homework because they do not understand something critical. This may be due to poor instruction, lack of clarity about the assignment, or daydreaming on the part of the student during an explanation. But, the result is that the homework is not complete. A reasonable and respectful policy will take these factors into account. In addition, teachers should ask students to document what they did before abandoning their homework: what approaches they tried, for example, the names of the students they phoned for help. Such a policy sends the message that perseverance and resourcefulness are important, so students should not give up at the first sign of trouble.
- *Teachers should coordinate major assignments*: Students are quick to notice when major assignments form two different courses are due on the same day, and they are not completely open to their teachers' suggestions that a little advance planning would mitigate the conflict. If a school wants students to give energy to the work they do outside of school, it makes sense or teachers in different departments to share their schedules for major assignments with one another. Students should certainly be expected to complete small daily assignments in many subjects, but major assignments should be coordinated.
- *Teachers should help parents help their children*: A school's staff should support a richer intellectual environment at home for students, independent of homework, by encouraging parental involvement. Educators should enlighten parents who do not recognize the educational value of regularly reading aloud to younger children or of asking them to set the table or sort the laundry. Older children can be asked to read bus schedules or road maps on car trios or to determine which brand of soap is the best bargain at the

supermarket skills that require higher-order thinking. And children of all ages benefit from conversation or keeping a journal. Educators should help parents to appreciate the value of these activities, so that they will encourage their children to take part in them.

General Policy Guidelines

School policies: The best way to ensure that everyone is informed of what is expected in terms of homework is for schools to have a written policy, which should be publicly available on request. Homework policies should set out clearly what the purposes of homework are, and should include information regarding:

- Developing home — school partnership.
- Consolidating and reinforcing skills and understanding.
- Extending school learning.

In primary schools, the focus of homework should be on the important skills of literacy and numeric. Regular reading at home, especially reading with parents, should be encouraged.

Older pupils in primary schools should be given other tasks such as finding out and preparing information as well as traditional writing tasks. This helps to ease the transfer to secondary schools.

In the upper echelons of secondary schools, the emphasis is on following up work done in class, consolidating learning and completing examination projects. However, schools should ensure as far as possible that homework amounts to more than merely finishing off tasks begun at school.

In ensuring an effective homework policy, the school should consider the questions set out below:

- What is appropriate homework for all pupils, especially for those with special educational needs?
- Who should ensure that the homework demands on pupils are consistent and manageable? At secondary level, a homework timetable is recommended and the

amounts of homework should be co-ordinated by subject and pastoral staff.

- How can pupils be encouraged to value homework and how are parents to be involved in the process?
- How are the setting and completion of homework tasks to be monitored? An increasing number of schools use homework diaries or planners, signed by parents and teachers.
- What facilities other than the home can be made available for homework?
- What system for monitoring and evaluating both the whole school and individual subject policies would be appropriate?
- How much time for homework should be required, bearing in mind that other activities, such as extra-curricular sport and music, are also important in supporting pupils' studies.

Schools may also wish to include study support and out-of-school-hours learning in the homework policy. Study support activities may include homework and study clubs, sports and outdoor activities, community volunteering and mentoring.

Implementation:

- Schools will ensure that homework is an integral part of the curriculum and is planned and prepared alongside all other programmes of learning.
- Pupils will record and ensure their understanding of the homework tasks and demonstrate a commitment to spending an allocated time doing the tasks set and handing the work back on time.
- Parents or guardians will encourage and monitor homework and inform the school if an issue arises.

Evaluation:

Homework policy should be promoted throughout the school, and its implementation and effectiveness should be reviewed annually. This is to ensure that teachers and parents are completely clear about what is expected of pupils in terms of homework and how it should be organized and managed.

Samples of Homework Policy:

Format One:

Guidelines for the Homework Assignment and Responsibilities of Students, Staff and Parents:

Purpose:

- To reaffirm that homework is considered beneficial and important in a student's overall educational programmes.

Process and Content:

- The instructional plan for each school should address the way in which the school and each teacher will make appropriate use of homework in carrying out the school's responsibility to assure that each child receives a thorough and systematic grounding in basic skills.
- Parents and students are to be informed school, and classroom homework policy.
- Homework assignments are to relate directly to instructional objectives.
- Homework assignments should account for individual differences among students.
- Homework activities should include opportunities for concept and skill development through review and enrichment experiences. Activities involving aesthetic appreciation or expression and use of community and natural resources shall also be valid homework assignments.
- Completed homework assignments are to be reviewed by the teacher and appropriate instructional follow-up shall occur.
- Homework should not be assigned on designated religious holidays when students are absent because of religious observances.

- Homework can be made up with teacher assistance where necessary when the pupil is absent because of other school-related activities.
- Homework procedures are to be monitored in accordance with administrative regulation.

Review:

- This policy will be reviewed every two years in accordance with the school policy review process.

Grades one to three: When a homework assignment is missing a note will be written in the student's plan book. After five assignments are missing in one quarter, an official letter will be sent home requiring a parent's signature and a parent's plan of action for solving the problem. A copy of this letter will be placed in the student's file. If a student cannot complete homework due to an emergency or illness, the parent should write a letter explaining such matters. Acceptance of the excuse is contingent upon the teacher. Approximate time for homework assignments in grades one and two should be half an hour per day. In grade three, the approximate time should be quarter to one hour to one hour per day.

Grades four to eight: Each student will be given hundred points for each subject at the beginning of each quarter. For each assignment that is not complete, accurate and neat, as defined by the teachers, five points will be deducted from the hundred points. In addition, a note will be averaged into the student's quarter grade. Once a student misses four assignments in one subject in one quarter, an official letter will be sent home requiring a parent's signature and the parent's plan of action for solving the problem. A copy of this letter will be placed in the student's file. Homework assignments may also be graded. For each day these assignments are late, an additional ten per cent will be deducted off the grade of that assignment (in addition to the five points already deducted from the hundred points). No extra credit will be given for missed homework at any time. If a student cannot complete homework due to an emergency or illness, the parent should write a letter explaining such matters. Acceptance of the excuse is contingent on the teacher. Students in grades four, five and six can expect approximately one to one and half hour of homework per day, while those in grades seven and eight should expect one and half hour to two hours per day.

Absent work: All work missed because of an excused absence is due the day after the child returns. If a child misses several days in a row, they will be allowed a reasonable amount of time to make up the work, as decided by the teachers. It is the responsibility of the student and parents to find out what work was missed.

Cooper (1994) suggests that each elementary, middle and high school should instil a homework policy that addresses the needs of its students and the community as a whole. He emphasises a need for policies characterised by clarity that, at the same time, allow for communication and flexibility. He proposes strong guidelines for increasing the clarity of homework assignments and controlling homework load, especially for students with a different teacher for each subject.

A Recommended homework policy for schools: The frequency and duration of homework assignments should be further specified to reflect local school and community circumstances.

In schools where different teachers teach different subjects, teachers should know:

- What days of the week are available to them for assignments?
- How much daily homework time should be spent on their subject?

Administrators should:

- Communicate the school homework policies to parents.
- Monitor the implementation of the policy.
- Coordinate the scheduling of homework among different subjects, if needed.

Teachers should clearly state:

- How the assignment is related to the topic under study?

- The purpose of the assignment.
- How the assignment might best be carried out?
- What the student must do to demonstrate the assignment has been completed.

Cooper (2001) continues to expand on his proposed guidelines for effective homework policies by further defining the amount of homework each student should be doing based on his and others theory of the presence of a strong grade-level effect. Cooper proposes, "The amount and type of homework students do should depend on their development level and the quality of their support at home."

Homework needs to be assigned with a specific goal in mind i.e., not only as work to keep the child busy and to encourage more than simple repetition of what was done in class. Rather, homework should be an extension of classroom experiences. It should require students to build on the knowledge acquired during the school day by applying the concepts to other areas of interest or by encouraging the child to take the next step on his or her own (Julie Hancock, 2001).

Homework assignments need to be designed and implemented with each student's best interest in mind. Individual differences not only in academic abilities, but also in home life situations, need to be considered at all times. Researchers have placed considerable emphasis on the necessity of assigning homework that is age/grade level appropriate. As educators, we need to continuously adjust our teaching strategies, including the use of homework to the individual needs, abilities and life circumstances of our students.

The homework component of the policy should have the following key points:

- While framing homework policy, each and every point must be clearly worded so that it may not create any confusion in the minds of any stakeholders of homework such as parents, teachers, students and even administrators.

- Homework should be well planned, age-appropriate and provide meaningful opportunity for learning enhancement or skill practice.
- Schools are expected to develop policies that define the amount of homework completed at different grade levels. The intent is to provide students with regular, meaningful homework.
- Teachers are expected to co-ordinate homework assignments so that on an average a student's homework falls within the expected time frame. This may mean that different teachers are assigning homework on different nights. Despite efforts to coordinate homework, there may be times that a student's homework may exceed or be less than the expected average.
- Homework may be varied where appropriate to provide support for learning differences.
- Guided practice in the classroom may be a useful methodology, however, guided practice should not replace homework to be completed outside of the classroom.
- Homework expectations should be clearly shared with students and parents through communications such as parent letters, rubrics, and assignment guidelines.
- A homework chart should be posted in the classroom to help all students organize their assignments and enable them to take responsibility for their own work.
- Sometimes homework should not be typically graded and therefore having the child try their best on their own is much more helpful for the teachers.
- A missed assignment should be counted as one that was not tried or not turned-in—not one that was tried but is not correct.
- Homework policies and practices should not be rigid. It should be designed to promote learning. If it is rigid, the consequences of incomplete homework should not be punitive.

- Homework policies and practices should be flexible and designed to promote student learning. Consequences for incomplete homework should be firm but respectful.
- Students should have an opportunity to contribute to the development of the policies.

Late Work Policy

For any assignment turned in after the due date, the highest grade possible is a "D". All late work is due no later than 1 week after the due date. In order to assess child's understanding of the skill, all late assignments must be completed and submitted. Work turned in later than one week after the due date will not be accepted and be given a grade of zero. Students must be notified of missing assignments and make arrangements in the case of excused absences. Students are given a planner to help them keep track of assignments and will be asked to have them signed daily by parents if missing work becomes a problem.

What Teachers, Students and Parents Need to Do

Teachers will:

- Teach and support good study habits and time management skills.
- Provide meaningful feedback regarding homework.
- Notify parents if homework is not being completed consistently.
- Suggest opportunities for extended learning.
- Communicate expectations throughout the year.

Students will:

- Understand homework expectations and ask for clarification, when needed.
- Be aware of due dates and turn in assignments on time.
- Request make-up work when absent.
- Practice good study habits and produce quality work.

- Students in grades 5 and 6 will complete, take home and use their daily planners consistently.

Parents will:

- Establish a consistent, organized place for homework to be done.
- Help their children establish a consistent homework schedule.
- Encourage, motivate and prompt their children without completing the homework for them.
- Support teacher efforts and student responsibility.
- Check the student planner daily.
- Contact the child's teacher immediately if the child is consistently spending an excessive amount of time on homework.

Format Two:

Guidelines for the Homework Assignment and Responsibilities of Students, Staff and Parents:

I. Purpose:

Homework contributes toward building responsibility, self-discipline and lifelong learning habits. It is the intention of the School staff to assign relevant, challenging and meaningful homework assignments that reinforce classroom-learning objectives. Homework should provide students with the opportunity to apply information they have learned, complete unfinished class assignments, and develop independence. Homework grades are modified based on students' individual needs.

Homework assignments include:

- **Practice** exercises to follow classroom instruction.
- **Preview** assignments to prepare for subsequent lessons.
- **Extension** assignments to transfer new skills or concepts to new situations.
- **Creative** activities to integrate many skills toward the production of a response or product.

II. Time:

Actual time required to complete assignments will vary with each student's study habits, academic skills, and selected course load. If the child is spending an inordinate amount of time doing homework, the parents should contact child's teachers. Students are encouraged to pursue non-assigned, independent, leisure reading.

III. Late Work Policies:

Students are expected to turn work in on time. Students who turn in late assignments on a consistent basis will receive any of the following based upon individual teacher discretion or grade level policy.

- No credit
- Partial credit
- Missed reward activity
- Communication with parents
- After school detention

Students who miss homework because of an absence will receive the opportunity to make up missed work. Students are given one calendar day for each day absent plus one extra day to turn in their work. It is the students' responsibility to get work missed due to illness or absence.

IV. Major Projects:

Major Projects include research reports, book reports, major essays, and other assignments teachers designate as major projects.

Responsibilities of Staff:

- Assign relevant, challenging and meaningful homework that reinforces classroom learning.
- Give clear instructions and make sure students understand the purpose.
- Give feedback and/or correct homework.
- Communicate with other teachers.

- Involve parents and contact them if a pattern of late or incomplete homework develops.

Responsibilities of Parents:

- Set a regular, uninterrupted study time each day.
- Establish a quiet, well-lit study area.
- Monitor students' organization and daily list of assignments in their agenda.
- Help student work to find the answer, not just get it done.
- Be supportive when the student gets frustrated with difficult assignments.
- Contact teacher to stay well informed about the student's learning process.

Responsibilities of Students:

- Write down assignments in the "Delano Middle School Student Agenda."
- Be sure all assignments are clear; don't be afraid to ask questions if necessary.
- Set aside a regular time for studying.
- Find a quiet, well-lit study area.
- Work on homework independently whenever possible, so that it reflects student ability.
- Produce quality work.
- Make sure assignments are done according to the given instructions and completed on time.

Format Three:

Guidelines for the Homework Assignment and Responsibilities of Students, Staff and Parents:

- All homework assignment descriptions will be posted on the class web page. Please check the announcements periodically in case there are any corrections, clarifications, or modifications made after the original posting.

- You should work alone.
- All the assignment should be turned.
- If you are working in a pair, the two partners may collaborate on all parts of the homework and write their solutions together.
- Assignments are to be turned in on the due dates with the following included:
  - Date
  - Class
  - Name
  - Section
  - To keep assignments from separating, put them in a folder or securely staple sheets together.
- Each assignment should be clearly labelled, and all assignments should be in proper order and legible.
- There are no late provisions for homework.
- Checked homework will usually be returned with feedbacks.
- We plan to also make all of your scores available on a secure basis via the class web page.

Format Four:

Guidelines for the Homework Assignment and Responsibilities of Students, Staff and Parents:

- The purpose of the assignments is to have students practice with the concepts and ideas discussed in class and for them to demonstrate that they understand them.
- The teacher is not interested if the student can get the answer by skipping half the steps.
- In writing an answer to a problem, students' target audience is a fellow student, so problems should be presented in a way that someone who is learning the material for the first time would understand your steps taken to solve a problem.

- The grader reserves the right to assign zero points if the homework fails to adhere to any of the following guidelines.

(a) Write neatly.

(b) Keep it organized. In part, this means keep it sequential — the grader should not have to search for problems out of order nor follow arrows all over the page to grade a problem. Additionally, you should clearly label the beginning of each section, staple the sections in order, and be consistent if you put the problems in columns. And lastly, clearly indicate that your answer, and nothing else in the problem, is what is to be considered when grading.

- Homework grade is divided into two parts:
  - *Completion of assignment*: One third of the points are based on completion of all the assigned problems. A genuine attempt must be made to solve all of the exercises to receive full credit.
  - *Content*: Two-thirds of the points are based on the correctness of a few problems (usually three) selected by the grader. Points are awarded based on the following two items, in order of importance: work and correctness of problem. Students must show an appropriate amount of work that demonstrates their knowledge and understanding of the material. Even if students are unable to complete the problem, partial credit can be given for at least explaining where they believe the error in their calculations has occurred and how it might be fixed.
- At the end of the quarter, the lowest homework score will be dropped. The main purpose of this policy is to allow for extenuating circumstances where an assignment cannot be turned in due to illness or other reasons.
- **Late Assignments:** A grading assignment turned in late is not a simple matter. The only way for the grader to assign points fairly is to grade all the assignments in one sitting. It takes at least twice the normal amount of time

to grade an assignment turned in late as opposed to grading it with all the other assignments. In addition, the criteria for partial credit may change somewhat from week to week. As a consequence, a late assignment will only be checked for completeness, meaning that none of the problems will be graded. Thus, students will receive a maximum of one third of the points possible for the assignment.

Key Points to Note:

- Parents and students must be informed that they will be handed over a Homework Policy form at the beginning of the school year. They should be instructed to read it over (with your child), discuss its importance; both the parents and the student should sign it, and return the bottom portion to the class teacher.
- All students are required to have an assignment sheet in their notebook at all times which lists all assignments. Parents should review these sheets weekly.
- Students who have not completed homework by the due date will be assigned one-half hour detention that will be used to make up missed work.
- Late work will result in a lower grade. If homework is not turned in consistently, parents will be notified and asked to begin checking and signing completed homework each night.
- If students still choose not to do their homework, they also choose to lose certain privileges. Students may make up missed work the next day, with a grade reduction on the assignment, but will not be required to attend detention.
- Students having difficulty completing homework may be required to attend tutorial sessions.

Among all the three formats, the homework policy-makers at school can adopt whichever is sound good and suits to its learning atmosphere or a school can develop its own homework policy according to its own educational policy and practices. It is suggested that it will definitely be highly rewarding if the schools develop or their own homework policy, as it will be a great learning experience.

A Sample of Letter:

Dated:...........

Dear Parents,

We have adopted a homework policy that will stress the value of student work and assist them in finishing work that may be crucial to their understanding of what is taught in class. Our homework help sessions are an after-school programme designed to help students complete current work (remember that late homework is not accepted) and receive tutorial help when needed.

The 7th grade policy for homework is as follows:

1. *On a weekly basis, teachers will meet to discuss missing homework. If a student is missing three assignments in a quarter, a phone call will be made to the parent informing you of what work was not completed.*
2. *When a student is missing five assignments within a quarter, a list of these will be given to the Head of Homework Guidance Centre to schedule homework help session. If a student does not attend the session, he/she will be assigned an In-School Suspension the following day to complete their new assignments.*
3. *Any student who comes to the session without proper materials, wastes time, or is disruptive will be sent home. The student may then be assigned another help session at Head's (Homework Guidance Centre) direction.*
4. *Homework during these sessions must be current work and must receive a passing grade to be considered complete.*
5. *The policy for absences remains in place and students are expected to make up their work as in the past.*

We have instituted this policy to encourage our students to meet their homework responsibilities. We appreciate your support in carrying out this policy. Please return the bottom portion of this paper to indicate that you have received and read this plan.

Sincerely,

XYZ

....

Note: *Please sign and return it to the teacher.*

I have received and read the 7th Grade Homework Policy for the 2005-2006 school year.

Parent/Guardian's Signature with date:

Student's Signature with date:

3.6 HOMEWORK RESOURCES

Homework Resources are:

- *Homework Guidance and Counselling Centre*: Every school should have Homework Guidance and Counselling Centre where teachers will inform the Centre head as what has been given to the students as homework assignments in the class. Also, this centre will guide and help the students as well as parents regarding homework difficulties. The centre must keep all the necessary information regarding homework, such as homework policy, homework timetables, information regarding various homework resources etc. At the centre,

Homework Counsellors should be available to discuss a student or parent concern and coordinate communication with multiple teachers. They can also refer parents and children to additional resources. The Homework Guidance and Counselling Centre phone numbers, e-mail and website addresses should be available to all — students, parents, teachers, etc.

- *Homework Club*: Every school should have Homework Club.
- *Before-school and After-school help*: There should be provision to have before-school and after-school help for the students.
- *Tutoring*: The Homework Guidance and Counselling Centre should provide names of potential tutors. Occasionally, peer tutoring by an older student should be used.
- *Internet*: Every school should have Internet connection facility.
- *Website and e-mail*: Teachers should post homework assignments on the Internet and/or make their e-mail addresses available.
- *Homework Hotlines*: There are a number of homework hotlines on the Internet that may be of benefit to students with occasional questions or problems regarding homework. If there is none, the Govt., Board of education, schools or District administration must establish one.
- Alternative Education Support Services such as
  - Time management skills
  - Study skills
  - Test preparation
  - Organizational skill
  - Specific content/or skill support
  - Social skills

- Extra homework help on daily or long-term assignments (research materials)
- Teaching assistants and teacher aides
- Social skills
- Librarians
- Social workers

STAKEHOLDERS AND HOMEWORK

4

4.1 HOMEWORK AND PARENTS

Home is the first school and parents are teachers, supporters, learners and advocates of their children, whether the parents view themselves in those roles or not. Children learnt how to eat, talk, sit up and walk long before entering school. In fact, many children learn more from their parents in the first five years of life than they do from school in the next ten years. A parents' role as 'teacher' does not end when the child enters school rather responsibility increases. Some of them that a parents' responsibility continues when their child enters school include:

- Talking about what is being done at school,
- Providing time and place for doing homework,
- Reading with a child,
- Making sure homework is understood and finished,
- Continuing to learn how to help.

In short, parents must adopt MMF model i.e. be a motivator, a monitor and a facilitator. When as a parent we are acting as a motivator, we must act positively about homework about our child's capabilities, and reinforce the importance of school. Our child will definitely acquire our very positive attitudes. We must offer word of encouragement. We must try to answer questions with a question that would make a child think of the answer on his/her own. When as a parent we are acting as a monitor, we must see and watch our child for signs of failure and frustration and suggest short breaks. Also, provide guidance not answers. Make sure that needed materials are available such as pencils, paper, dictionary etc. When as a parent we are acting as a facilitator, we must see that our child also needs a reasonably quiet, well lit place to do homework. We should try to provide facilities, which may help them to do his/her homework so that maximum learning may take place.

The research demonstrates that parental attitudes toward homework play an important role in their children's education. Thus, it is required on our part as a parent to have positive attitude if homework is to be beneficial. Following are the ways that can be tried by the parents to help their children:

- Taking an active interest in homework.
- Ensuring that there is time set aside for homework.
- Encouraging and supporting students to complete homework.
- Providing, where possible, a dedicated place and desk or homework and study.
- Encouraging their children to read and take an interest in current events.
- Assisting teachers to monitor homework by signing completed homework if requested and being aware of the amount of homework set.
- Communicating with teachers any concerns about the nature of homework and their children's approach to the homework.
- Alerting the school to any domestic or co-curricular activities which may need to be taken into consideration when homework is being set or corrected.

In spite of all sincere efforts and proper involvement there are the times when we as parents are unhappy with the type of assignments when our children bring home. Parents should discuss such concerns with the teacher. However, it is not realistic to expect every assignment to be a prize winner. With some creativity, parents may be able to enrich an assignment.

Parents should not believe in waiting for the shock of that first big assignment. Initially, a child to participate in activities that may appear petty like writing the grocery list, or measuring ingredients for cookies, promotes learning outside the classroom. Parents can tell their kids a hundred times a week that education is important, and have little impact. But, when they show by their actions, that they need and value what schools teach, the message gets through.

In some cases it has been found that parents do the homework on the behalf of students. Doing our child's homework for him undermines the whole purpose of homework. Being overly involved creates other problems, too. Sometimes parents explain things so differently from the teacher; the child gets even more confused. There is need to first discussing the assignment with the teacher. Graydon (1999) says, "keeping tabs on homework is a tangible way for parents to assess progress.... There are no report card surprises for parents who are involved". In the enthusiasm to help our child, we should not overstep the line. We should always make our child to help to think and this is possible when the child gets the first opportunity to do.

Sometimes children are found frustrated with their homework. Children's frustration with homework is often linked to either not understanding the instructions or not having mastered the required skills. If the problem seems to be that they honestly cannot do it, discuss the situation with the teacher, who should offer additional help or suggestions.

If they simply do not want to do the work, think twice before resorting to rewards. Bribery can be tricky. Thus, as far as possible, try to avoid it. Instead of bribery, try to determine the underlying cause of the problem — he/she may be tired or hungry or need you to sit near him or her while he/she works.

Discussing difficulties with the teacher is valuable for both parents and teachers, and given the reporting of many children, it may be the only way to find out what really is happening. If a talk with the teacher does not satisfy us as a parent, we should ask the principal to arbitrate. Overall, when we take the time and trouble to offer support and encouragement we should send a strong signal that homework is important. And while homework may not always be a sweet experience for children, it need not be a bitter lesson.

How can parents help their child with his or her homework?

Whenever we want to help our child with his or her homework, we all need to identify answers (either by ourselves or by discussing with experts, researchers, the teachers concerned or by scanning the best literature available) to the following questions that are quite helpful and insightful in nature. The questions are:

- Why do teachers give homework?
- How can we help with homework?
- How much help should we give?
- What if we do not understand our child's assignment?
- How much time should our children spend each night on homework?
- Can our children do homework while listening to music or watching television?
- Do teachers really want me to ask them questions about homework?
- Our child seems bored by homework. Is this normal?
- What if our child still is not turning homework in?
- Should we reward our child for doing homework?

Many parents are uncomfortable helping their children with homework. The parent may feel that his or her own proficiency is being tested, and may be nervous about appearing uncertain (let alone ignorant) in front of his/her child. Because of this discomfort, there is a tendency for the parents to overcompensate by solving the problem, telling the child the right answer and then explaining the solution. Frequently, this is not the best way to promote the child's learning. The first thing to remember is that this is our child's homework not ours.

There are some more ideas to be tried out:

We should ask our child to see his/her class notes or class work. This may help us to understand what the child is expected to know as well as what he or she is not. It is important to understand what is not expected, because we probably will not want to explore those areas. Let us say for example, our child is working on a geometry problem that would be easily solved using the Pythagorean theorem, but that method has not yet been discussed with the child. While using the Pythagorean Theorem might be the easiest way for us to solve the problem, it will be less confusing for us to help our child using the method that he or she is currently studying.

We should ask our child to list what he or she knows about the problem. The child should be asked to sort through the information and figure out together what information would be useful in solving the problem and what information is not needed. He or she should be asked to try organizing the information provided in the problem using one of the following strategies:

(a) Draw a diagram.
(b) Make a list.
(c) Eliminate possibilities.
(d) Look for a pattern.
(e) Guess and check.
(f) Solve an easier, related problem.
(g) Work backward.

As parents we must want homework, and if homework keeps parents in touch with the programme of the school, then it is the abolition of homework — not its presence — that most threatens parents' interest.

Show that the parent think education and homework are important

Our child needs to know that their parents and adults close to them think homework is important. If they know their parents care, children have a good reason to complete assignments and turn them in on time. There is a lot that parents can do to show that they value education and homework. Parents must provide enough time to finish homework. If there is not sufficient time, the parents may ask their child to drop some outside activity. At any cost homework must be a high priority.

Parents should encourage their child to make a schedule, to write out and put it in a place where they will see it often. Some families have a required amount of time that children must devote to homework or some other learning activity each school night (the length of time can vary depending upon the child's age). For example, if the eight standard child knows that he or she is expected to spend an hour doing homework, reading or visiting the library, he or she may be less likely to rush through assignments so that he or she can watch a television programme of his or her choice. A required amount of time may also discourage him or her from 'forgetting' to bring home assignments and help him or her adjust to a routine.

Pick a place: A study area should have lots of light; supplies close by, and be fairly quiet. A study area should not have to be fancy. A desk in the bedroom is nice, but for many youngsters the kitchen table or a corner of the living room works just fine. The child may enjoy decorating a special study corner. A plant, a brightly coloured container to hold pencils and some favourite artwork taped to the walls can make study time more pleasant.

Remove distractions: Turn off the television and discourage social telephone calls during homework time. (A call to a classmate about an assignment may however, be helpful.) Some youngsters work well with quiet background music, but loud noise from the stereo or radio is not ok. If parents are living in a small or noisy household, try having all family members take part in a quiet activity during homework time. Parents may need to take a noisy toddler outside or into another room to play. In short:

- Set aside a regular time for homework every day.
- Make sure that the child has the necessary things at hand.
- Find a fairly quiet, well lit place for the child to study.

- Set a positive example by reading or writing yourself.
- Keep a close contact with the child's teacher.

Conclusively, our consistent message should be: "Homework is important to your success in school, and I expect homework to be done appropriately." It is critical that the child understands that we place as much importance on homework being done each night as we do on the child going to school each day.

Show the value of learning

The whole purpose of assigning the homework is to facilitate learning. By establishing a family routine of talking about the value of learning of which homework is one means of accomplishing this goal, the meaning of homework shifts from just a boring task requiring repetitive effort to a valuable system for learning. We must not forget that homework activities help children develop essential skills for independent learning.

A simple way of valuable learning is to discuss learning at the dinner table. Our children will then understand that education and learning are values. For example, each child can take turns talking about what was learned that day at school. We can talk about work experiences or current events. These discussions might also involve problems or conflicts that were encountered at school or work, solutions that were chosen and questions that remain. Such discussions communicate that effort, interests and even making mistakes are vital in the process of learning and growing. The encouragement of interests will be significant in moving the child ahead in the long-term than the specific grades or marks the child receives. Additional ideas to emphasize the value of learning might include trips to museums, family vacations that involve learning (e.g., a trip to Capital). The gist is this that when the child perceives homework as another aspect of the learning process he or she will take a more active, responsible role in homework as well as in all school activities.

Provide supplies and identify resources

For starters, parents should collect pencils, pens, erasers, writing paper, an assignment book and a dictionary. Other things that might be helpful include glue, a staple, paper clips, maps, a calculator, a pencil sharpener, tape, scissors, a ruler, index cards, a thesaurus and an almanac. Keep these items together in one place if possible. If we cannot provide our child with needed supplies, check with the teacher school guidance counsellor, or principal about possible sources of assistance.

We should try to minimize time lost when the child is looking for items necessary for completing assignments. For this, we can create a homework survival kit — a box that holds critical supplies. For books and other information resources, check with the school library or local public library, which may have, homework centres designed especially to assist children with school assignments.

These days many schools have computers in classrooms and many households have personal computers. Computer may be a great help to complete home assignments. If we can afford, we all should have computers. However, we do not have to have a computer in our home in order for our child to complete homework assignments successfully.

We may want to ask the teacher to explain school policy about the use of computers or any special equipment of homework. Certainly, computers can be a great learning tool and helpful for some assignments. They can be used for word processing and on-line reference resources as well as educational programmes where the child can use the school computers. And many public libraries make computers available to children.

Set a good example

Children are more likely to study if they see us reading, writing and doing things that require thought and effort on our part. Talk with the child about what we are reading and writing even if it is something as simple as making the grocery list. Tell them about what we do at work. Encourage activities that support learning — for example, educational games, library visits, walks in the neighbourhood, trips to the zoo or museums, and chores that teach a sense of responsibility.

Show an interest

We should make time to take our child to the library to check out materials needed for homework (and for fun too) and read with our child as often as we can. Talk about school and learning activities in family conversations. Ask the child what was discussed in class that day. If he or she doesn't have much to say, try another approach. For example, ask the child to read aloud a story he or she wrote or discuss the results of a science experiment.

Another good way to show our interest is to attend school activities, such as parent-teacher meetings, shows and sport events. If we can, volunteer to help in the classroom or at special events. Getting to know some classmates and other parents not only show we are interested but helps build a network of support for our child and us.

Convince your child what you expect

Convince the child that you have been looking at the child's homework assignment and you know that the child can do a better job. The child must not rush through his or her assignments. Tell the child that you want him or her to take his or her time and do the best work he or she can. "Sloppy work with a lot of mistakes, or unfinished work is not acceptable. I will check your work each night when you are done."

Institute mandatory homework time

If we find that the child rushes through the homework assignment most frequently, it is probably because the faster it is done the more time he or she will have to spend with friends or watch TV. Mandatory homework time takes away these advantages of getting homework done as fast as possible.

Mandatory homework time means that a child must use the 'entire' schedule daily homework time for homework reading. If two hours is allotted each night, then the extra time must be used reviewing, practicing or reading, without exception.

Monitor assignments

Children are more likely to complete assignments successfully when parents monitor homework. How closely we need to monitor depends upon the age of our child, how independent he or she is and how well he or she does in school. Whatever the age of our child, if assignments are not getting done satisfactorily, more supervision is needed. Here are some good ways to monitor assignments:

Ask about the school's homework policy: At the start of the school year, ask the teacher: what kinds of assignments will be given?, how long are children expected to take to complete them?, how does the teacher want you to be involved? etc. Teachers' expectations vary. Ask the child's teacher what we as a parent should do. Should we just check to make sure the assignment is done, or should we do something more? Some teachers want parents to go over the homework and point out errors, while other ask parents to simply check to make sure the assignment is completed. It is also a good idea to ask the teacher to call if any problems with homework come up.

Be available: Elementary school students often like to have someone in the same room when working on assignments in case they have questions. If the child will be cared for by someone else, talk to that person about what we expect regarding homework. For an older child, if no one will be around, let him know you want him or her to begin work before we get home and call to remind him or her if necessary.

Look over completed assignments: It is usually a good idea to check to see that our elementary school child has finished his or her assignments. If the junior high school child is having trouble finishing assignment, check him or her too. If we are not there when an assignment is finished, look it over when we get home. After the teacher returns completed homework, read the comments to see if the child has done the assignments satisfactorily.

In short:

- Keep track of what the child's homework assignments are, how long they should take, and how the teacher wants us to be involved.
- Make sure that the assignments are started and completed.
- Read any of the comments the teacher makes about the child's work when the assignments are returned.

Monitor Television viewing

Nowadays children on an average spend far more time watching television than they do completing homework. In many homes, more homework gets done when television time is limited. Once we and our child have worked out a homework schedule, take time to discuss how much television and what programmes he or she can watch. It is worth noting that television can be a learning tool. Look for programmes that relate to what our child is studying in school such as programmes on history or science or dramatizations of children's literature. When we can watch shows with the child, discuss them and encourage follow-up activities such as reading or a trip to the museum. In short:

- Try to make sure that the child completes his or her homework before the television goes on.

Provide guidance

The basic rule is "Don't do the assignments yourself". It is not parents' homework — it is our child's. Doing assignments for the child won't help him or her understand and use information. And it won't help him or her become confident in his or her own abilities.

It can be hard for parents to let children work through problems alone and learn from their mistakes. It is also hard to know where to draw the line between supporting and doing. Different teachers have different ideas about the best way for parents to provide guidance. Here are a few suggestions with which most teachers agree:

Figure out how the child learns best : We must understand that *learning to like the process of learning is more important than marks or grades or even learning*. Thus, if we understand something about the style of learning that suits the child, it will be easier for us to help him/her. If we have never thought about this style, observe the child. See if he or she works better alone or with someone else. If the child gets more done when working with someone else, he or she may want to complete some assignments with a brother or sister or a classmate. (Some homework, however, is meant to be done alone. Check with the teacher if we aren't sure.)

Other things to consider about learning style: We should try to find out:

1. Does our child learn things best when he or she can see them? If so, drawing a picture or a chart may help with some assignments. After reading his or her mathematics book, he or she may not remember the difference between the two different types of angles or triangles. But, by drawing a picture of chart, he or she can remember it easily.
2. Does the child learn things best when he or she can hear them? He or she may need to listen to a story or have directions read to him. Too much written material or too many pictures or charts may confuse him or her.
3. Does your child understand best when he or she can handle them? An apple cut four or six or eight ways can help children learn fractions.

In short, try to discover how the child learns best:

- With someone else or alone?
- By seeing the concept in front of him/her?
- By hearing it or talking it through?
- By hands-on experience of the concept?

Help your child get organized

Please keep in mind that patience and step-by-step management are vital to developing organizational skills in the child. To threaten them — can unravel the child. To overwhelm the child — can immobilize the child. Yet, to rescue the child can undermine the self-confidence in child's ability to take charge of his or her life. The most promising approach is to model and coach. Coach the child by slowly and gradually building upon his or her progress and appreciating every step the child takes towards independence.

As mentioned earlier, it is a good idea to set a regular time for children to do homework. Put up a calendar in a lace where we can see it often and record assignments on it. If child is not able to write yet, then do it for him until he can do it himself or herself. Writing out assignments will get him or her used to the idea of keeping track of what is due and when. We may want to use an assignment book instead of a calendar. A bag for books will make it easier to carry homework to and from school. Homework folders in which youngsters can tuck their assignments for safekeeping help many children stay organized.

In short:

- Provide a place where things can be kept when the child is finished with his or her work.
- Help the child develop good study habits by helping him or her to pace big projects.
- Discuss the child's homework with him or her.
- Make sure that he or she understands what is expected and what needs to be.

Encourage good study habits

Teachers generally give students tips on how to study. But, it takes time and practice to develop good habits. We can reinforce these habits at home. For example, help your child structure time in order to complete assignments. For instance, if ninth standard student has a physics report due in two weeks, discuss all the steps he or she needs to take to complete it in time, including: selecting a topic; doing the research by looking up books and other material on the topic and taking notes; figure out what questions to discuss; drafting an outline; writing a rough draft and revising and completing the final draft.

Encourage the child to write down how much time she or he expects to spend on each step. Help the child get started when he or she has to do research reports or other big assignments. Encourage him or her to use the library. If he or she is not sure where to begin have him or her ask the librarian for suggestions. If she or he is using a computer for on-line reference resources — whether the computer is at home, school or the library — make sure he or she is getting whatever help he or she need to use it properly. After the child has done the research, listen while he or she tells us the points he or she wants to make in the report.

Give practice tests. Help the third standard child for a spelling test by saying the words while he or she writes them down. Then have her correct her own test.

Help the child avoid last minute cramming. Review with the child how to study for his or her social studies test well before it is to be given. We can have his or her work out a schedule of what he or she need to do to, make up a practice test, and write down answers to the questions he or she is made up. We should talk with the child about how to take a test. Make it sure that she or he understands how important it is to read the instructions carefully and to keep track of the time and avoid spending too much time on any one question.

Talk about the assignments

We must ask our child questions. Talking can help him think through an assignment and break it down into small, workable parts. Here are some sample questions: Do you understand what you are supposed to do? After the child has read the instructions, ask to tell you in his or her own words what the assignment is about. (If the child cannot read yet, the teacher may have sent home instructions that we can read to him or her.) Some schools might have homework hotlines, we can call for assignments in case the child misplaced a paper or was absent that day. If the child does not understand the instructions, read them with him or her and talk about the assignment. Are there words he or she does not understand? How he or she can find out what they mean? If neither you nor the child understands an assignment, call a classmate or contact the teacher.

What do we need to do finish the assignment?

The child may want to talk through the steps with you (or make a written list of them, if he or she is able to), as described in the section above on good study habits.

See if the child needs to learn more, for example, about subtracting fractions before he or she can do her assignment. If we understand the subject ourselves, we may want to work through some examples with the child. But, with all certainty, we must let the child do the assignment himself or herself.

Does the answer make sense to us?

Sometimes the response to a mathematics problem does not seem logical, or the meaning of a paragraph the child has written is unclear. If that is the case, the child may need to check over the mathematics problem or revise the paragraph. If the child is still confused, ask:

- How far have you gotten on the assignment? Let us try to figure out where you are having a problem.
- Do you need to revive your notes (or re-read a chapter in your textbook) before you do the assignment?
- Are you still having problems? Maybe it would help to take a break or have a snack.

Adapting homework assignments to maximize child's strength

If the child is a poor reader and the purpose of a social studies assignment is to learn about a specific time in history, forcing the child to struggle through reading the material is not productive. This will not only lead the child to dislike reading, but history as well. In other words, it is important not to allow the child's skill weaknesses to interfere when the purpose of an assignment is gaining knowledge. If our child experiences problems with reading or reading speed, either read the material to or with the child. These compensations will allow the child to focus on understanding and comprehending the material. It is a little known that the majority of children struggling to burn to read could read to learn if they could decode. That is, when read to, the majority of children with reading disabilities comprehend at a level consistent with their age and development.

In contrast, when increasing reading speed and proficiency is the goal of the homework assignment then the child must read independently. At all ability levels, when asked to read out loud to their parents, children improve reading skills above and beyond those who do not have this reading experience.

One of the key factors to help the child with homework is to understand lesson objectives. If the lesson objective is solving mathematics story problems, then reading the problems to the child or allowing the child to use a calculator does not represent a change of lesson objective. However, if the objective is mathematics calculation and the child computes mathematics problems using a calculator, then a change of lesson objective has been made. In this case, allowing the child to check mathematics calculations with a calculator could be used as a reinforcer after a certain number of problems are completed; such an activity would not involve changing the lesson objective.

The lesson objective in homework assignments may not always be apparent. If we are familiar with the subject area, then we may have an idea of the general contents objective. If we read the instructions provided to the child we can probably figure out what skills the assignment is targeting. For instance, if the child was asked to read about Japan and then answer questions about geography, such an assignment targets understanding the culture rather than reading. If the child was asked to re-write sentences using commas, the assignment is directed at developing punctuation rules rather than handwriting. Finally, if the child is asked to read about a time in history but has difficulty with specific works, rather than stopping and having the child sound out or look up these words, which is distracting, it is suggested that we should read the words for the child, such that the focus can remain on gaining information from reading. If these suggestions make sense, we can be generally confident that we will be able to quickly understand and discern the objectives of child's homework, if these examples are not apparent, it is suggested that we must take the time to strengthen the skills in the area. One way to begin this process is to communicate with the child's teachers to make certain that we as parents understand the assigned objectives of homework.

A system of returning homework to school on time

Although most parents devote most much of their energy to helping children complete assignments, some children struggle to develop the independent skills necessary just to return completed homework. When homework is completed, children usually are able to access enjoyable activities. Thus, it is not surprising that some children view the completion of homework rather than turning the homework in as the end point in the process. They may have completed homework at school or at home but misplaced it, misread the teacher's instructions to turn it in, or forget to bring the assignment to school.

It is important to help the child develop the independent habits to return homework to school. Children who forget to bring homework to school should first try keeping a homework folder in their backpack. When the homework is finished each night, help the child develop the habit of putting the homework in the folder and in the backpack at night to be returned to school the next day. We may need to remind our child in the morning to look over assignments due that day.

When children experience difficulty remembering to turn in assignments, we may also want to contact our child's teacher to develop a system to cue the child to turn homework in. Eventually this cuing system can be reduced. A teacher can be asked to place a green (any colour) index card on the child's desk each morning. The card could be a cue to remind the students to place their homework in the green pin. The card may be placed in a smaller bin next to the homework. The act is that after contacting the teacher, we should work out an agreed upon plan such that each party agrees and understands what the other will be doing to help the child to develop more effective skills so that he or she may return the completed assignments compulsorily.

A more independent system to remind our child to remember to turn homework is to create an assignment-tracking sheet. Our child should develop the skill to mark assignments in each subject when they are due and whether a book, notebook, or worksheet needs to be brought home to complete the assignment. This assignment sheet could serve as a checklist for assignments that have tuned in, as well.

With the increasing use of technology, homework at time can be faxed or e-mailed to school. The Internet may be used to access the teacher's online files if the school has such a system in place. This system allows us to check the child's progress on a weekly basis.

Give praise generously

People of all ages respond to praise. And children need encouragement from the people whose opinions they value most — their parents. "Good first draft of your book report"! or "You have done a great job" can go a long way toward motivating the child to complete assignments.

Children also need to know when they have not done their best work. Make criticism constructive. Instead of telling a fourth standard child, "You aren't going to hand in that mess are you?" try, "The teacher will understand your ideas better if you use your best handwriting." Then give praise when a neat version is completed.

Consistently praise the child, everyday for what he or she is doing well. Don't save the praise for good marks/grades only. Tell the child specifically what you like about what the child is doing or what they have done. A hug or pat on the shoulder increases the messages impact.

Use incentives to get children motivated. Where praise is not enough, sometimes we have to use other incentives to get them motivated. An incentive is something that motivates a child into action. Once the child starts working on his/her own, the rewards can be phased out but make sure to keep up the praise. It is important to note that rewards do not have to be expensive. More than anything, the child wants his or her parents' attention. Rewards may include watching his or her favourite movie together, going and getting ice-cream or going to the park.

Talk with someone at school to resolve problems

Homework hassles can often be avoided when parents/guardians value, monitor and guide their children's work on assignments. But, sometimes helping in these ways is not enough. Problems are still come up. If they do, the schools, teachers, parents, and students may need to work together to resolve them.

Share concerns with the teacher

We as parents may want to contact the teacher if —

- Our child refuses to do his or her assignments, even though we have tried hard to get him or her to do them;
- Instructions are unclear;
- We cannot seem to help our child get organized to finish the assignments;
- We cannot provide needed supplies or materials;
- Neither we nor our child can understand the purpose of assignments;
- The assignments are often too hard or too easy;
- The homework is assigned in uneven amounts—for instance, no homework is given on a particular day but on the very other day four of the child's teachers all make big assignments that are due the next day; or
- The child has missed school and needs to make up assignments.

In some cases, the school guidance counsellor may be helpful in resolving such problems.

Work with the school

Communication between teachers and parents is very important in solving homework problems. Here are some important things to remember:

- Talk with teachers early in the school year. Get acquainted before problems arise, and let teachers know that you want to be kept informed. Most elementary schools and many secondary schools invite parents to come to parent-teacher meetings or open houses. If the child's school does not provide such opportunities, call the teacher to set up a meeting.
- Let the teacher know if there are any family issues that might be affecting the child's performance or ability to meet with the teacher as soon as you are aware that a problem has arisen.
- If the child consistently continues to have problems completing his or her homework, work together with the teacher to develop a home/school contact plan that will fit in with our schedule and will help our child develop the skills needed to complete the homework assignments in a timely manner.
- Communicate with the child's teacher early, before a potential problem gets out of hand.
- Contact the teacher as soon as we suspect our child has a homework problem (as well as when you think he is having any major problems with his schoolwork). Schools have a responsibility to keep parents informed and we have a right to be upset if we do not find out until report-card time that our child is having difficulties. On the other hand, sometimes parents figure out that a problem exists before the teacher does. By alerting the teacher, we can work together to solve a problem in its early stages.
- Request a meeting with the teacher to discuss homework problems. Tell him briefly why you want to meet. You might say, "Ankur is having trouble with his mathematics homework. I am worried about why he can't finish the problems and what we might do to help him." Do not go straight to the principal without giving the teacher a chance to work out the problem with you and your child.

- Approach the teacher with a cooperative spirit. Believe that the teacher wants to help you and your child, even if you disagree about something. It is hard to solve problems if teachers and parents view each other as enemies.
- If we have a complaint, try not to put the teacher on the defensive. For example, avoid saying that we think the assignments are terrible even if we think so. We might say, "I am glad Ankit is learning to add and subtract in the first grade, but he does not want to do his mathematics work sheets. Can we find another way for him to learn the same material?" This might encourage the teacher to let Ankit (and the rest of his classmates) try another approach. Perhaps he can learn addition and subtraction by moving around coins, sticks or shells.
- Let the teacher know if the child is bored with assignments or finds them too hard or too easy. (Teachers also like to know when children are particularly excited about an assignment.) Of course, not all homework assignments can be expected to interest the child and be perfectly suited to him or her. Teachers just do not have time to tailor homework to the individual needs of each student night after night. However, most teachers want to assign homework that children enjoy and can complete successfully, and they welcome feedback from parents.
- Many times homework can be structured so that a wide range of children will find assignments interesting. For example: different approaches to the same topic or lesson can be offered to students; extra assignments can be given to students who want more challenge; and specialized assignments can be given to students having trouble in a particular area.
- While meeting with the teacher, explain what you think is going on. Also, tell the teacher if you do not know what the problem is. Sometimes a child's version of what is going on is not the same as the teacher's version. For example, our child may tell us that the teacher never

explains assignments, so he or she can understand them. But, the teacher may tell you that the child is not paying attention when assignments are given.

Work out a way to solve or lessen the problem

The strategy will depend on what the problem is, how severe it is and the needs of our child. For instance: *Is the homework often too hard*? May be the child has fallen behind and will need extra help from a teacher, parent or tutor to catch up. *Does the child need to make up a lot of work because of absences*? The first step might be working out a schedule with the teacher. *Has your child been diagnosed with a learning disability or is one suspected*? If so, we will need to make sure the child gets extra help and the teacher may need to adjust some assignments.

As parents we should not forget that homework could bring together children, parents, and teachers in a common effort to improve student learning. The younger the child is when we start to do the kinds of activities suggested above, the better.

Helping the child with homework is an opportunity to improve our child's chances of doing well in school and life. By helping the child with homework, we can help him or her learn important lessons about discipline and responsibility. We can open up lines of communication — between us and our child, and us and the school. We are in a unique position to help the child make connections between schoolwork and the "real world", and thereby bring meaning (and some fun) to our child's homework experience.

Whether we succeed in doing all of the activities suggested is not what is most important. What is most important is that we are willing to take the time and make the effort to be involved in our child's attempt to complete homework assignments and education successfully.

Certain precautional measures

Avoid doing the homework yourself: Some parents are found doing the homework themselves for the child forgetting that the homework is for the child not for the parents. This may get good marks or grades for the parent, but it sure does not do much for the child's learning process. If the child gets an 'A' on some homework that was mostly done by the parent or the tutor, the grades or marks look good, but the child did not learn anything other than it must be ok to cheat on homework. The whole purpose of homework assignments gets defeated. In doing the homework for the child, parents are robbing him off what could be a horizon widening experience. It is better for the child to do just part of an assignment well than for we to do it. Here are several additional suggestions if we are unsure about how to provide doing the work for the child:

(a) Help the child get started.
(b) Make certain that the child understands the directions for each assignment.
(c) Help the child prioritize the specific tasks to be completed.
(d) Provide the child with magic markers to highlight important information.
(e) Provide incentives (e.g., preferred activities when each task is completed).
(f) Communicate with the child's teacher to make certain the length of assignment is reasonable for the child.
(g) Be available to help the child when specific problems arise.

One of the favourite techniques is to request that the child be the teacher and teach us about the assignment while we pretend to be the child. It is well recognized that we all learn and retain information more efficiently when we teach that we have learned to someone else. This process will also indicate how well our child has mastered the material by the ways in which he or she teaches it to us.

Do not protect the child from the consequences of minor mistakes: If the child forgets his or her homework, let it happen, do not run up to school with it! The lesson can be to better organize at home so that if it is not forgotten again. The reduction of credit for tardiness is not a life threatening consequences.

Avoid excessive corrections: An excessive correction reduces everyone's motivation and increases feelings of low self-worth. Be sensitive when providing feedback. Learning occurs in safe environments where children do not need to defend their actions, strategies or opinions. Some correction is necessary for children to learn what does not work or is inefficient. Most times, however, children will arrive at their own understanding. This process can be accelerated by asking the child if he or she can think of another way to complete the task. We can then guide the child specifically by asking him or her to think of a faster, more careful way, or a way that a tricky fox would use, etc. However, when accuracy is important and there is only one correct answer or response, we can look for similarities in mistakes and point these out as on type. Alternatively we can point out a single mistake and ask the child to find others of the same type and fix them all at one time (one error rather than many). Children also learn well from general rules to prevent errors.

We must remember that our child will learn best when we point out what is correct and what is better than the last time. This is particularly true of children who have suffered from "success deprivation" at school. A good rule is to provide at least three compliments for every correction. In general, praising effort is better and more realistic than falsely claiming the work, as a whole is outstanding. Keep in mind that our child may compare his or her work to others. For this reason we should encourage comparisons of the child's work with his or her previous work and effort — not with others. These self-comparisons will improve long-term motivation.

We must listen carefully to what our child has to say about homework and be sensitive to any feelings of frustration. It is important for us to view homework and education within the total fabric of our child's life. Education requires children to be generalists who are good at everything.

Remain task oriented: It is important for us to accept the feelings of frustration our child may occasionally have with homework. It is also important that we then redirect our child back to the current task, explaining what need to be done and how to best to do it. Feeling frustrated, at times, is a normal occurrence of life. Nonetheless, if it occurs too frequently, there is a problem to be addressed. In response, if we become irritable or angry, our behaviour will only heighten our anxiety as well as our child's frustration. Perhaps a good initial question to ask our child is "In what ways do you want help?"

If the child drags his or her heels in getting his or her work done, any one of variety of reasons is possible. Maybe, he does not understand the work. Maybe it is dull and boring to him or her. Possibly, he is assigned too much work too much of time. Possibly he or she sees no benefit or reason in doing it. Probably he or she would rather be doing something else. Maybe he or she is a person who tends to procrastinate, whatever the job.

Before we decide he or she is just fooling around, we need to check the kind of assignments he or she is bringing home. If his or her assignments consist of work not finished during the day, he or she needs to finish the work at home. Certainly; but his or her non-performance in school will be an additional problem to be addressed.

If he or she does not seem to understand what he or she is supposed to be doing, a little boost from us may put him under right track; or it may become evident that he or she is in over his or her head academically. In this case he or she should be at a different level of instruction. That is yet a different problem, one that may call for a meeting with his or her teacher.

Some children have a very low threshold of tolerance for written assignments. They involuntarily freeze up when faced with what seems to them an overwhelming task. The problem can be severe enough to hamper seriously a child progress in school. Some students are completely bold over by routine written assignments. They are so intimidated they will not begin, as would finish only a few words before giving up.

A parent can help with this problem in the homework situation by encouraging him or her every time he or she writes a few words. Using the technique of shaping, we can help our child to learn to increase his or her capacity for written or other kinds of words. This may involve rewarding for very small increments to begin with and gradually working up. It takes a certain amount of time, and a lot of patience. It is to be remembered that it is our own child whom we are teaching how to live successfully.

But, if it is only a matter of disinterest and boredom, there are some other things that we as parents can do. If we can teach him or her, the habit of getting his or her homework done promptly, he or she will be learning a precious lesson whether or not the homework itself provides any learning value. His or her reward comes from getting an undesirable job out of the way so that he or she can enjoy the rest of the day. It will be even better if the child can learn to take some sense of achievement in the homework itself.

When we are mulling over incentives, it is wise to be aware that a young child does not comprehend the long-term goals. A young child does not connect what is happening now with what is going to happen six weeks from now when report cards come out. The importance of passing not likely to mean anything to him or her until the grades or marks arrives.

Some young children seem naturally to take pride in good grades or marks on daily papers, spelling tests and so forth, while others need to be encouraged to develop the sense of pride. If our child is having some problem regarding homework, it is likely the child is in the latter group. Therefore, in coming up with incentives, be aware the incentive, or reward, forgetting his or her work done will have to be immediate. Warm praise, perhaps an activity or special treat at supper, when the day's assignments are finished, will be more effective than a big blow-out when report cards come out several weeks down the line. The most abhorable kind of incentive to the child comes in the form of paying a child in money for doing these kinds of things. We may get results, but we *will also be teaching our child that money is the ultimate*.

Some other possible incentives in addition to praise — always include praise — might be such thing as going to play immediately after a specified work has been done. May be the child could watch his or her favourite television programme if he or she is finished by the time it comes on. *We know our child, so we can probably think of others that will apply to him or her*.

The pivotal thing to remember is the reward we devise needs to come immediately after getting some of the work done. If our child is having a short attention span, we may need to provide the reward after getting a small amount done and the more when the more is done. We should not stretch the amount of work required more than the child is capable of attending to at one sitting. *Again, we know our child best so we should use our own sense of judgement*.

While dealing an older child we have to modify our tactics. The principles are same, but the things that are rewarding are changed. It is good to remember that to an adolescent, a parent's approval is probably is very important, but it is not cool to admit it.

At this point let us look again at a statement from the perspective of responsibility. To teach a child to be responsible, we should give him or her all the choices he or she is able to make and allow him or her to have the complete consequences of those choices.

Homework is an aspect of responsibility which we should want it to be our child's responsibility not ours. We are talking about an older child now, one who is capable of understanding the consequences of not doing one's homework. These include such things as trouble the next day at school from the teacher, leading to possible failure at the end of the term. However, if the child is consistently not doing it, the results are the same as if he or she does not understand.

Lectures about how a child is not going to pass the quarterly or half yearly, and how he will never be able to get a good job if he or she does not make good grades/marks, and how the child will probably end up as an old man sitting under bridges, will probably fall deaf years. Some immediate consequences will have to be introduced if we have to get results. We should not nag or fuss. We should see that pleasant thing happen as soon as the homework is done. We should find the way to make it pleasant while it is being done.

It would be probably wise to make it a rule that no TV, Computer games, other desirable activities are to be indulged in until the homework is completed. Here we are making the desired activity contingent on him or her fulfilling his or her responsibility. That is different from punishment, which would be something like taking it away from him or her tonight because he or she did not do it last night. It is to be remembered that punishment is the least effective way of controlling behaviour. We may want our child to connect fulfilment of responsibility with reward rather than punishment. If we keep on saying that he/she is not going to get to watch such and such if he or she does not hurry up and finish his or her homework, we are making it their responsibility. There is no need to say anything. We should simply keep control of the consequences.

It has been noticed that sometimes each teacher behaves as if his or her assignments were the only ones the student has to worry about. Night after night of this is a real burden to some children. As it is stated earlier, in such cases, the child deserves a short break every now and then during the evening. Any one can be overwhelmed by the prospect of a whole evening of work with no relief. An older child, able to grasp the concept of long-term reward, might also benefit from some kind of special treat at the end of gruelling week, provided he or she has done his or her best.

Meeting with the teachers will also be rewarding in case of overwhelming amounts of homework. It may not do much good, but on the other hand they might not realise what total load the student is receiving. Teachers are conscientious people who genuinely want to teach the pupils. If they can understand that they are teaching to their pupils to hate school and schoolwork, they might be able to see it differently. It is worth a try.

If the child has any conscience about the necessity of homework, he or she will still procrastinate getting it done. But, he or she will be feeling the heavy burden of the incomplete work hanging over his or her head. Thus, it is advised to help the child to do the assignments as soon as they are assigned rather than wait until they are due. If we can instil this idea in our child early, the child will not have to suffer through school because of the heavy burden of unfinished work hanging over the child's head.

If problems persist regarding incompletion of homework, talk with the child about their day at school. Give the child an opportunity to unwind and regroup as school is the child's 'work' and like adults, the child might need some time to regroup before he or she is ready to share the day with us.

Ask open-ended questions. A yes/no question will most likely generate a yes/no answer. We should get into the habit of wording our questions in such a way that our child would need to respond with a phrase or a sentence. Some emphasis might include:

- "Tell me three things that happened while you were at school today."
- "Tell me what games you played during recess today? Whom did you play with?"
- "What was the best part of the story that the teacher read to you today?"
- "Who was in the story?"
- "Tell me about the picture you like the best."

Play a guessing game: Small children love to play games where they are 'teaching' adults. We can tap into that by planning a fun "guessing game" with them. It could go something like this:

"Let's see now. You got to school and then you went to lunch...."

"You didn't go to lunch first?...."

"Oh, so you had reading first! What did you do in reading then?"

"That's really great...oh and then you had lunch...not yet?"

"Ah, Oral Language! And tell me what you did in oral language?"

"The teacher wrote WHAT on the board?"

"...It sounds like you had a fun and interesting day...."

"Oh, you forgot to tell me what you had for lunch!"

The ABCs for Parents

- Ask your child about the school day.
- Begin your child's day with a nourishing breakfast.
- Congratulate your child for doing well.
- Discuss homework with your child.
- Encourage your child to read.
- Find a quiet place for your child to study.
- Give your child your responsibility.
- Include your child in making simply family decisions.
- Join a library with your child.
- Keep your child on a schedule that includes exercise and sleep.
- Limit TV viewing by selecting programmes with your child.
- Make the time you spend with your child special.
- Notice and discuss changes in child's behaviour.
- Offer to help the child organize school papers.
- Provide the child with good role models.
- Question the activities your child shares with friends.

- Respect your child's right to have opinions different from yours.
- Share an interest or a hobby with the child.
- Take time to listen to your child.
- Urge the child to say "NO"! to unwanted touching.
- Visit places of interest with your child.
- Work with the child to set up rules of behaviour.
- Xerox results by encouraging the child to do better.
- Zoom through these ABC again and again!

Parental Involvement in Homework

Parents' involvement with homework as well as monitoring after school activities will help them and their child begin to build a homework alliance. As a member of the homework team, parents will need to encourage their child's schoolwork. They may listen to their child read, participate in learning games or storytelling and make themselves available as needed. Although during the adolescent years most students can complete homework independently, even during the secondary school years it is important for them to convey availability to their teen should problems arise with schoolwork. All of these activities have been reported to increase achievement, with the greatest gains made in reading skill for younger children. Parent's positive involvement will increase homework competition, school attendance, improve child's attitude towards school and decrease the likelihood their child will experience behavioural problems in school.

The research on direct parental involvement in children's homework shows:

- In general, parents want schools to set homework, although homework can be a cause of conflict between parents and children.
- Parents are more directly involved in homework when their children are younger. The degree and type of parental involvement in homework are related to cultural and socio-economic factors.

- Research indicated clear relationship between the amount of parental involvement in homework and pupil's achievement at school.
- Parental involvement in homework takes different forms, and these appear to have different relationships with pupil involvement. It is possible for parents to intervene in either appropriate or inappropriate ways.
- Research into specific reading initiatives indicates that parental involvements are not sufficient for success. Again, the type of involvement may be the key factor.
- Parent involvement can be used to speed up a child's learning.
- Homework can involve parents in the school process. It can enhance parents' appreciation of education.
- It can give them an opportunity to express attitude about the value of success in school.
- It can clarify for parents what is expected of students.
- It can give parents a firsthand idea of what students are learning and how well their child is doing in school.

Thus, parental involvement should include:

- Fostering a partnership with the teacher to further the education of the child.
- Serving as a coach, gradually allowing for more independent work.
- Creating a homework environment conducive to learning.

Some important questions to ask our child when we are told, "I don't have any homework":

1. Did you begin any assignments in class today that you need to finish tonight?
2. Do you have any specific homework assignments for tonight?
3. Do you have a test to prepare for?
4. Have you read to yourself the lessons discussed in class, and can you answer any questions at the end of the lesson?

5. Do you know the spelling and meaning of each of your assigned vocabulary words for every subject?
6. Do you know your mathematics facts (addition, subtraction, multiplication, and/or division) quickly by memory?
7. What is the title of the book you are reading? Tell me about it (characters, settings, problem, and resolution).
8. What letter are you practicing in cursive? Practice that letter and make up words, which contain that letter. Practice the entire alphabets.
9. Are there any art projects that need to be completed?
10. Do you have a favourite subject you can look up in the encyclopaedia and share with your class tomorrow?
11. Is there anything else related to school that you know you have to read or work on?

Above-mentioned questions are not sufficient in itself. Further questions can be added up in the above list as per the need and requirements as and when needed.

Parental involvement should include:

- To become familiar with the policies and guidelines of the child's school and teachers.
- To help the child establish home assignments assigned by the school as a high priority above social and recreational demands.
- Fostering a partnership with the teacher to further the education of the child.
- Serving as a coach, gradually allowing for more independent work.
- Creating a homework environment conducive to complete the assignments so that maximum learning may take place.
- Parents must make the child to realize that homework is an important element in the development of life-long learners. Thus, it must be completed on time, accurately and neatly.

- Helping the child develop a satisfactory study schedule that includes ample time to study regularly and to complete long- and short-term assignments.
- Recognise the value of various types of homework.
- To encourage independent work unless the assignment requires group or parental involvement.
- Accept each child's personal work and avoid comparisons with other persons and/or with other circumstances.
- Communicate with appropriate school personnel when the child experiences frequent difficulty in completing assignments.

To have proper and adequate involvement, parents should:

- Be familiar with the school's Homework Policy (if any) and teachers' expectations.
- Demonstrate a commitment to the Importance of Homework.
- Provide an appropriate study environment (i.e. time, materials, space and conditions).
- Motivate and give assistance to child.
- Provide feedback to the school regarding Homework.
- Maintain consistency with Homework practices.
- Share any concern we may have regarding the amount or type of homework.
- Encourage their child to take notes concerning homework assignments in case questions arise later at home.
- Provide a suitable area and the necessary tools to complete the homework assignments.
- Limit after-school activities to allow time for both homework and family activities.
- Monitor television viewing and establish a specific homework time.
- Plan a homework schedule with their child. Allow for free time when assignments are completed.

- Praise child's efforts. If questions arise about the assignments, and the child asks for help, ask him or her questions or work through an example rather than simply providing the answer.
- Go over homework assignments with the child, as younger children need more parental assistance with homework than older children. Do several problems or questions together and then observe the child doing the next or two.
- If the child is in elementary school, check completed assignments. At all levels, ask to look at homework once it has been marked and returned.
- Ask child's teachers about their homework policy and specific assignments.
- Offer praise first on work done before offering suggestions and corrections.
- Do not let the homework struggle dominate our relationship with our children. Homework is a part of school experience and not all of who they are.
- Be patient. Be kind. Take the time to teach the child that good homework habits can lead to greater academic success, self-confidence and self-reliance.

We must not forget that our task is to help our child feel successful and confident about doing homework irrespective of our roles as supervisor, teacher, cheerleader or mentor.

Now the question arises how to help the child? Following are some guidelines to keep in mind to support your child, and to help keep evenings a time for positive family interactions.

Creating a Time, Place and Plan

Homework needs to fit into the flow of the family. For some working at the kitchen table while dinner is being prepared can be fine, and for others having a designated place in our house to complete homework, away from family activity is the most productive. It is important to understand how our child is best able to work and concentrate.

Give the child choices regarding time and place. Some children are comfortable alone in their bedroom while others will choose the kitchen table. Important criterion:

- Study in the same place everyday.
- Do work on a hard surface.
- Ask yourself...can you concentrate there?
- Supplies should be at the fingertips.
- No distractions.

Have a regular time for dining homework, but be flexible. Take into account situations, sporting activities, hunger and level of energy. Homework time should neither be assigned late in the evening nor when the child is tired. Enforcing time schedule for homework is an effective way of increasing the number of assignments completed. However, when we do not monitor the time schedule, we may discover that the child will not maintain the schedule independently. Therefore, it is important for us to consistently enforce this schedule a family rule. We must remember that behaviour needs to be repeated many, many times before it becomes a habit or a routine. The younger the child, the more repetitions will be needed.

The child needs to learn effectively manage his or her time — both their free time and homework time for school and life success. Some tips:

- Prioritize the things — a good way to manage time.
- To make prioritize "to-do" list.
- List the activities from the time school gets out until bedtime.
- Prioritize homework assignments onto a to-do list.
- Use a calendar to keep track of dates and deadlines.
- To teach the child to record information in advance so they can plan for upcoming assignments and events.
- To encourage the child to design his or her own personalized calendar.

Preferably, homework should be completed immediately after a snack (or playtime) but before preferred activities (e.g., television). It is suggested that we must consider a number of short homework periods in the early afternoon interspersed with preferred activity times, especially for children with learning or attentional problems. A daily plan can be communicated to the child by a written or tape-recorded list of activities specifying times to be spent on homework, chores, and preferred activities. It is also suggested that we should develop a list of preferred activities with the child. These can be available when homework is completed. Preferred activities can be as simple as additional time prior to bedtime and can be used to increase the number of minutes children spend on homework. Certain snacks might also be offered as rewards for efforts directed towards homework completion. But, make certain that we spend a fixed amount of time with the child each week that is not dependent upon the quality of their behaviour of work.

Try not to deny access to an activity that may be an important "one time event" (e.g., the circus coming to town, the birthday party of a friend or relative). Make sure that the child has access to sports and recreational activities that are also not dependent on the quality of behaviour or homework.

How to make learning time management fun:

- Write the name of the month on top of twelve blank calendar pages. Put them in order in a folder, section of the notebook or on a bulletin board/wall.
- Go through each month and write the names of important events — tests, assignment dates, vacation dates, sports schedules, birthdays, party dates....
- Glue to a piece of construction paper and creatively decorate the background for each calendar to give it a "personal touch".
- Hole punch for notebook. If hanging, put holes at the top and string together with two loops of yarn. Then hang with paper clips.
- Each month, add important dates to your calendar.

Short-cut tips:

- Try colour coding events for 'at-a-glance' searching i.e. — write homework in red, tests in blue, vacation dates in green and so on.
- Make a weekly study plan: Use a weekly planner to remember all kinds of information. If the school has one — use it. Transfer important events from monthly calendar to weekly plan. Put all assignments and due dates in it. Frame and hang it for quick reference.
- Estimate how long assignments and activities will take. When a child can estimate the time it takes to complete a job, he or she can make good choices as to when to start. Only practice at estimation leads to accuracy.
- Break down big assignments into smaller parts to make time for each part. This prevents it from becoming overwhelming and discourages waiting to the last minute.

Also, have reasonable expectations of his or her work. Don't expect perfection. If our child asks us to check his or her homework, we should go ahead. If we find a mistake, say some thing like, "You might want to give this problem some more thought", in other words, put the responsibility back on him or her, but do not condemn her for errors. If there were many mistakes, it would be appropriate to say, "I see a number of mistakes here. I am sure you will catch them yourself if you go over the assignments one more time.

It will not be sufficient to pay adequate attention at home only. It is desirable on the part of the parents to make it sure that they have a clear understanding of the entire scope and sequence of curriculum for the year and of the homework requirements. This should be done at the beginning of the school year.

Why should parents be concerned about school homework?

- Lack of an established homework policy may place either insufficient or unrealistic demands on our child. Students may not be expected to work to capacity:

alternatively, they may receive too many assignments from different teachers on the same evening.

- Schools with homework policies tend to set guidelines for teachers to correct, grade or marks and return homework systematically to their students, thus reinforce learning.
- Schools with homework policies generally specify guidelines regarding what is expected from parents.
- School with homework policies tend to carefully design and provide homework assignments appropriate to each grade level.

If we really worry that our child's homework looks like busy work, talk with the teacher about the school's 'homework policy'. This policy should be very specific, and include information about what is expected from students and what role parents should play. Here it is suggested that *if the school (in which the child studies) doesn't have a policy, there is a need to work with school officials and parents' organiations to implement one*. If the school has already a policy of homework coordination across classes, the parents must have through acquaintances with that. Also, the parents should ask the school authority to communicate the policy to the parents and offer ways for parents to connect with teachers if problems come up.

From the above points it is clear that if the school has good homework policy then it is all right otherwise problem is evident. Thus, parents are required to be concerned with homework in general and with homework policy in particular. Also, it is found that students may not always view homework as a pleasant experience, but if the assignments serve a good purpose and parents reinforce the completion of the tasks, students will benefit by gaining higher grades/marks, better study habits, and a more positive attitude toward school and learning. Homework assignments give parents insight into the school curriculum and offer a greater opportunity for student learning.

How much help with homework is appropriate?

The most useful stance a parent can take is to be somewhat but not overly involved. The emphasis should be on helping the child, not on doing homework for them. Some useful strategies for becoming involved in their child's schoolwork include the following:

(a) *Communicate*: It is a good idea to get an understanding of what teachers expect of our child. Meet with the teacher early in the year to set a good precedent for facilitating communication, if need be.

(b) *Monitor*: Talk about the assignment so that the child can figure out what needs to be done. Reviewing a completed assignment is helpful. For younger children, it is appropriate to help them with their homework and closely monitor their progress.

(c) *Encourage*: Regardless of our child's age, never underestimate the importance and impact of our praise and encouragement on our child's success. Talking about an assignment and showing their interest in their child's schoolwork may also help their child maintain his or her motivation and interest.

(d) *Model behaviour*: Parent's beliefs and practices are very important influences on children's success. We should show that we think homework is important by providing a consistent time and place for it. Try and help the child to see homework as an opportunity, not a threat. We should never use homework as a punishment and do not exempt kids from homework as a reward. Both actions imply that homework is not fun and not part of the routine and send a message that can backfire on students, teachers and parents.

The amount of assistance the child requires with homework will be determined by his or her age and level of ability. Elementary school students, as well as those with learning problems will require more of our time, assistance and support than secondary students. Our assistance also depends on whether the homework assignments represent practicing a skill already mastered by our child or developing and mastering a new skill. The later will take more time on our part.

Most parents feel quite capable of providing assistance when the goal of homework is to practice previously learnt information. In contrast, many parents fell less capable assisting their child when new skills of problem-solving exercises have been assigned. When acquiring new information is the object of a homework lesson, it may be important for us to ask questions about the materials to summarize for the child any past strengths in that area and to ask the child as well as his or her teacher how can best be of assistance.

How can I help our child be ready for homework?

By focusing on certain skill areas we can help our child complete his or her homework with stress and frustration.

- As said earlier, choose a specified space and time to do homework. Make sure to remove all the distracters. We should help our child concentrate by turning off the television, by limiting personal telephone calls, and by setting a good example by reading and writing ourselves.
- Making sure that the child has got all the necessary tools and supplies needed to complete the work.
- Helping our child to set realistic goals regarding how long each assignment may take so that he or she knows that they will also have free time.

Some more homework tips for parents:

- Show an active interest in the child's homework assignments. Ask about the subject and the work to be done.
- Be a role model. Take the opportunity to read a book or newspapers while the child studies. Reading together helps create a learning atmosphere.
- Teach the child how to be organized. Be sure he or she keeps a homework assignment book.
- Eliminate as many distractions as possible during study time.

- Develop a strategy for dealing with homework. Find a plan that works for our family and stick with it.
- Try to relate the homework to our child's everyday life. For instance fractions and measurement can be learned as the child prepares a favourite food.
- Encourage the child to establish a regular time to do homework. Developing a schedule might help avoid procrastination.
- Meet with the child's teacher to discuss the nature of the approach to reading, spelling and other topics that the child is being taught.
- Make sure the child has a specific place to do homework that offers ample lighting, minimal noise and plenty of workspace. In other words, parents should provide an environment conducive to study.
- Provide continued interest and concern for the student's successful performance in school.
- Support the homework policy; request assignment for the student when absences are anticipated or when prolonged absences have occurred.
- Praise the child for successfully completing homework. *Nothing builds self-esteem like praise from parents.*
- Use a "Homework Contract" if the child has problems doing homework.
- This contract is a written and signed agreement between parents and their child that states:
    (a) The specific homework rules that must be followed,
    (b) The specific reward the child will receive for following the homework rule, and
    (c) The consequences that will occur if the child does not do homework appropriately.
- Stay involved and informed.
- Call some homework hotlines if there is any.

Parent Responsibilities

Do we start sweating when we ask our child about homework, knowing that the answer to his/her seemingly harmless question might create a war like situation in our home? Some parents try to avoid the question as long as they can, hoping to have a few more hours of peace until the nightly homework battles begin. Others tackle the problem head on and ask the question before the child has both feet through the door. Some parents may remain uninvolved. Others may get too involved, causing their child to become overly reliant on parents for homework assistance.

As a parent we must be involved in our child's learning. We have the responsibility to make sure our child is getting the best education possible and that the child is taking school seriously. Parental involvement in children's education is extremely important if we want our child to succeed in school. Their communication, guidance and support of their child in the homework process are essential if the value of good homework practice is to be realized.

First of all assure quality by providing appropriate levels of supervision:

- Check assignment notebook regularly.
- Help students prioritize assignments.
- Review work as it is completed.

Maximize educational benefits:

- Emphasize need and importance of homework when prioritize activities:
- Encourage student's independence in completing homework.
- Ask or answer questions that lead to understanding and not mere repetition.
- Encourage thoroughness.
- Encourage regular attendance.

Be active participants in communicating with the school:

- Write comments in the assignment notebook.

- Contact teachers, counsellors or the principal by phone or e-mail.
- Ask questions and seek information.

Parents must be familiar well with the homework resources:

- Homework Counselling Centre
- Homework club
- Source line
- Websites and e-mail
- Tutoring

Apart from above facts, parents are responsible for providing an environment, which fosters the development of long learning skills. This may include:

- Reviewing the success planner.
- Calling the homework hotline.

Parents will:

- Send the child to school each day, well rested, fed and with a positive outlook.
- Take an active interest in child's schooling. Ask specific questions about what happens at school each day and how the child feels about it.
- Try not to let any of our own negative experiences keep us from supporting and encouraging our child's learning.
- Allow the child to study in the way he or she learns best. For instance, some children work best when they are lying on the floor with background music playing.
- Work with their child to examine family schedules to allow time for homework.
- Provide an appropriate homework setting that motivates students to complete all assignments.
- Contact the teacher directly or encourage the student to seek help when students show that they are having difficulty with their assignments or when extenuating circumstances prevent a student from completing assignments. The Guidance and Counselling department

may also be contacted for resources to help their child with homework.

- Review with their child each teacher's homework guidance at the beginning of each course, sign it and have their child return it as requested.
- Encourage good homework practice. Assist them in organizing their commitments and try to establish a definitive time and place to do homework.
- Communicate to teachers when the parent feels the homework might be too difficult or too much or cannot be completed due to certain circumstances. Be willing to discuss this openly with the teacher and the child.
- Encourage the students to seek help, or contact the teacher directly when the student is having difficulty of any sort or any confusion.

Strategies

- Assist with establishing a work environment conducive to learning.
- Provide the resources necessary to do the work.
- Assist with effective use of the assignment notebook.
- Encourage students to keep homework, assignment sheets, and notes organized.
- Assist in the development of time management skills.
- Make certain that missed assignments are completed.
- When a student is absent for three or more days, contact the Homework Counselling Centre (if any).

How to help children struggling to manage difficult or long-term assignments

Children struggling to manage difficult or long-term assignments will need to develop self-management skills. Some children are overwhelmed by multi-steps projects or confusing assignments. Their first reaction is to ask for help or put the assignment off for another time. A number of strategies can help our child handle these types of assignments:

- *Underlining*: Use magic markers to highlight important parts of directions.
- Read all of the headings, table of contents, chapter questions and bolded words in reading assignments. Highlight or write them down if that helps. Highlight directions in any worksheet. If it is a mathematics sheet, highlight symbols and signs.
- Make lists of important words or concepts.
- Tell yourself brief summaries into a tape recorder. Play them back and listen carefully.

It is also suggested that review the child's assignments to determine if there are any long-term projects waiting to be completed. Help the child set up a schedule to complete the assignment in a step-by-step fashion. Children do not intuitively know how to simplify a large task into manageable steps. To help them with this process, it is useful to focus their attention on the main feature of the task (e.g. to outline, headings, words in italics or bold, the questions at the end or the beginning of the work). Based on just these general features of complex tasks or reading material, this strategy will help children reduce large amounts of information to topics, questions or categories.

There are other ways to reduce information or to make directions easier to understand. For example, children can use magic markers to not only highlight directions but key points as well. Once the child can identify the important points, he/she can use a different coloured marker to mark the supporting points. This strategy can also be used in listing to teachers' lectures. If notepaper were divided into three columns, students could take notes on the main points in column one, supporting points in column two and questions or thought in column three.

Finally, there are ways to reduce the amount of information that must be organized when telling or writing stories. We know that many children will write better stories if they have first drawn small pictures of the story events. One picture can be drawn in each of the squares created by folding a piece of paper into six to twelve parts. When children perceive a homework assignment as too difficult it becomes a self-fulfilling prophecy. The assignment immediately becomes even more difficult because the child perceives it as such. If the child gives up without reasonable effort or requesting help, he or she will feel increasingly more helpless and hopeless towards school. There is need to teach the child to question himself or herself: "What do I know?", What can I do?" and "Who can I ask for help?" *These questions will help the child develop the academic self-confidence and assertive skills necessary to successfully complete difficult or long-term assignments.*

Many demands placed upon today's families make it difficult for parents to take the time necessary to be involved on a daily basis. Teachers often complain that it is difficult for them to involve parents actively with children's homework. This problem may result from parents' busy schedules but can also be the result of lack of certainty about the role they should play in the homework process. In most cases it is not the result of disinterest. Let it be assured that whatever problems arise, there are many different ways parents can establish an effective homework alliance.

How to help child make a dull or boring homework task more enjoyable

It would be wonderful in life if every activity were interesting as per our wish. But, our children and we as parents know that is not the case. Sometimes we have to work on boring homework task more enjoyable. First, increase rewards our child will obtain after finishing a dull task. For instance, what activities can our child look forward to? What snacks, games, or phone calls will our child make once this task is completed? Setting our sights on enjoyable activities once required tasks are done is a most effective form of self-motivation. Helping our child develop this capacity to delay or use a gratifying task as a reward for completing more mundane or boring tasks, will help our child become an effective, independent learner as well as efficient at completing homework. Secondly, try and change a boring task into something that is more interesting or even into a game. Encourage the child to be creative; play beat the cock or offer incentives for accurately completed work. Turn practice time for repetitive activities, such as learning to spell or master mathematics facts into "television game shows".

Many parents assume that their children do not like all kinds of homework. However, most children can describe their preferences. We must try to find out what is our child's favourite and least favourite homework activity? For this, we can develop a small questionnaire, which will help us and our children develop a better understanding of the kinds of homework they enjoy most and those assignments that may be more difficult to complete and will require additional incentive. It is suggested that the parents and child complete the questionnaire and discuss interests and preferences.

Homework Preferences Questionnaire

- Your Homework style/preferences..................
- Check those you prefer: Give examples of preferences.

.....................Drill and practice.

.....................Studying for tests.

.....................Reports.

Projects. What kinds do you like?

1. ....
2. ....
3. ....

Outside of classroom assignments. What kinds do you like?

1. ....
2. ....

Providing options and choice in workspace for homework

The way our child and we structure the homework conditions (e.g., place for homework, noise, light, television, availability of resources) has been found to play an important role in predicting homework preference. In fact, these issues have been found to be even more important checking and assigning homework. We should consider experimenting with a variety of locations and noise levels to decide what works best for our child. *A quiet isolated setting is not necessary the best for everyone.* It may surprise us to learn that children can complete homework and perform well in a variety of positions and places. Remember, homework is not like medicine. It does not have to taste bad to be good for us. In fact, the more pleasant we can make the surrounding study conditions, schedules and materials, the more likely our child will approach homework positively.

Setting to complete homework is best selected by our child because optional conditions in trying out different places different tasks. A tote tray containing all essential materials for homework (e.g., markers, ruler, scissors) can be portable and yet be used to keep all essential materials together.

How and where does our child complete homework best? It is suggested that we should create an experiment to discover this process. Ask the child to suggest three different places (e.g., kitchen table, on the bed, on the bedroom floor, at a desk, in the family room on the couch) and conditions for each (music, television or silence). We should allow our child the opportunity to complete homework under these differing conditions over a several weeks. Together we can then decide best which type of homework is best completed under which condition and in which location.

What to do when the child doesn't understand the homework

It is common for the child to become frustrated when he or she does not have a clear understanding of the material presented in class. Confusion about assignment is a common reason for incomplete homework. When the child is confused about the homework he or she can either ask for help, struggle on his or her own and eventually find a solution, give up or avoid the assignment to altogether. Confusion is more likely to occur during new tasks or when a new concept has been presented at school.

If the child dawdles over homework, one of the first things we should do is check to make sure the child understands the assignment. Sometimes the child is found resistant to accept that he or she is confused and refuses to seek help as this situation may embarrass him or her. If we find that the problem is a result of our child's confusion or that reflects poor ability, it is essential that our child's teacher and we develop a system to communicate clearly and consistently about homework assignments. Such a system might include:

- Colour coded homework folders to help remain organized (e.g. different colour folder for work going home and different colour for work coming back to school).
- Write homework assignment down using a coloured pencil so that our child's teacher can quickly locate and review what has been written before our child leaves school.
- Ask the teacher to assign a homework buddy. At the end of a period or day our child and a buddy can make certain that they each understand the assignment and what must be done that evening. If there is disagreement they can seek clarification from the teacher.
- If understanding written assignment is a problem, try other forms of communication. For example, reduce the information by using highlights to underline the important parts.
- Consider the possibility that our child's difficulty understanding directions for homework may be part of a larger problem related to a learning disability. When the problem persists, seek a screening from a school or community based professional.
- Consider that the same problems that cause our child to experience difficulty understanding homework instructions may also impair his or her ability to follow instructions in other situations in class. This may include taking tests. Our child may require direct instruction to learn effective test taking skills and listening strategies.

What to do when the child takes too long to complete homework

Most of the child starts his or her homework without difficulty. Some find it increasingly difficult, however, to remain on task long enough to complete homework. In these households, parents send a great deal of time getting their child to refocus attention to homework. In severe cases it can take many more hours than it should to complete homework. Needless to say, this can be extremely frustrating for both parents and children. Homework sessions become battlegrounds. A tug of war develops between parents who want homework completed and the child who does his or her best to avoid working.

Children may experience difficulty remaining on task to complete homework for a number of reasons. Some children simply struggle to sustain attention for independent activities. Others may be confused about the assignment and become lost as they begin working. Still others find homework boring and unmotivated to earn good grades.

Parents typically react to this kind of problem by keeping a close watch over their children during homework time. They help the child get started and supervise work closely. Whenever the child goes off task the parent reminds the child to return to work. The child may take the prompt as nagging and work for a short period of time but with increasing frequency move off task. Thus, a dance of dysfunction develops during homework time between parent and child.

Let us examine why this type of interaction is usually unproductive. When we prompt about homework, our child may return to task to get us to stop prompting. As long as the child is on task we should stop prompting. As long as we prompt the homework gets done. However the children do the homework for the wrong reason. They are working to eliminate the pressure we place on them. Each time we engage in this process the likelihood has increased that the process will be repeated. Unfortunately our children are not learning independent homework skills and we are placed in the position of becoming long-term homework grades.

The first step to end this cycle is to focus our attention on the positive aspects of our child behaviour rather than the negative. We should try the following:

- Accept that some children work at their own pace. Help the child understand that as well. Reinforce him or her with praise and rewards for engaging in homework even for short period of time.
- Encourage the child to work for longer periods independently by establishing work time or work production goals. A work time goal might be a specific number of minutes of on task behaviour, which then earns a reward when achieved. A work production goal might be a specific number of examples completed that earns a reward when achieved. Gradually extend work time or work production goals to increase the child's length of independent work. Continue to provide consistent, frequent positive reinforcement.
- Avoid failing into the nagging trap when our child is off task. Make an effort to ignore the negative, waiting for the opportune moment to reinforce the positive.
- Finally, it can be suggested that do not allow the child to have favoured or preferred activities such as watching television until homework goals are accomplished.

What to do when our child rushes through homework and makes careless errors

Some children work through homework quickly and are capable of doing a thorough, correct job. None of us would consider this a problem. However others rush to complete homework and make numerous, careless errors, hand in sloppy work or fail to pay attention to direction. These children must learn to work at a slower pace and check their assignments for accuracy. We should make certain that we explore the possibility that rushing through work is not a coping strategy our child develops because he or she does not understand, lacks the ability to complete the work, or lacks confidence. If the child sacrifices homework accuracy for speed, we can try the following:

- Review homework assignments nightly, checking for thoroughness, neatness and accuracy. Encourage the child to correct mistakes.
- Encourage the child to underline or highlight important works or phrases in the directions portion of an assignment to make certain the directions were read.
- Emphasize that we want our child to do his or her best work on homework not the fastest work.
- Help the child develop self-monitoring skills by checking for errors in spelling, punctuation, neatness, calculations, correct headings etc. Provide additional bonus privileges if we find the child has completed work neatly and accurately.
- Without favoured privileges until we are satisfied our child has put forth the best effort possible and has completed homework accurately. However, if we suspect errors are due to poor understanding rather than hasty completion, make certain we provide assistance as needed.
- Finally, we should not forget that some children experience difficulty with handwriting due to visual motor problems. This may make it an arduous endeavour for them to write neatly. Asking them to re-do homework and to be neater is often fruitless. If this is the case for our child, overlook neatness and thoroughness. For some assignments creative ideas and interesting ideas and interesting plots are more important initially than grammar or handwriting. Make certain we understand the lesson objective. Finally, when children experience significant visual motor problems consider allowing them to begin using a computer to complete assignments, even during the elementary grades.

What parents should know about homework assignments

Believe it or not, little attention is devoted to the topic of homework in teacher education. The homework practices of most teachers are developed on the job. When assigning homework, teachers must consider at least three factors:

- Instructions are clear and understood by all students.
- Assignments are meaningful and within the ability range of all students.
- How assignments will be reviewed, returned and explained to students.

To some extent our child's problems with homework may stem from the manner in which the teacher assigns, explains and reviews homework. By understanding these concepts we can speak with our child's teachers about how their homework practices could best meet the needs of our child. Take a moment and complete the homework tips for Teachers Checklist. It is designed to help parents identify the practices our child's teacher uses in assigning homework. This checklist is meant for the parent. But, it may aid us if we choose to offer suggestions to the child's teachers. If we are certain how to answer a question, check with the child or the child's teacher.

Homework Tips for Teachers Checklist

1. Does the teacher provide the purpose of an assignment?

   ....Yes.........No.............Don't know.

2. Is the due date provided?

   ....Yes.........No.............Don't know.

3. Are materials necessary to successfully complete the assignment recommended?

   ....Yes.........No.............Don't know.

4. Are the requirements for good performance explained, including the steps necessary for a long-term assignment or a project?

   ....Yes.........No.............Don't know.

5. Is there a system in place for students to obtain help when needed?

   ....Yes.........No.............Don't know.

6. Does the teacher provide time at the end of class for students to compare their understanding of homework assignments?

   ....Yes.........No.............Don't know.

7. Does the teacher ask students to repeat the assignments in their own words?

   ....Yes.........No.............Don't know.

8. Does the teacher provide time for students to begin their assignments in class at joined desks or tables?

   ....Yes.........No.............Don't know.

9. Does the teacher require students to rewrite or repeat directions before beginning written assignments?

   ....Yes.........No.............Don't know.

10. Is there a system in place whereby students can ask for help if they do not understand written instructions?

    ....Yes.........No.............Don't know.

11. Are students taught a system to highlight instructions with coloured markers?

    ....Yes.........No.............Don't know.

12. Does the teacher provide an outline on a weekly or monthly basis of assignments and deadlines?

    ....Yes.........No.............Don't know.

13. Does the teacher have a system to make certain that students have assignment books, homework planners or homework buddies to call in the event of problems?

    ....Yes.........No.............Don't know.

14. Does the teacher offer assignments at the beginning of the class rather than at the end when students may be thinking about recess or lunch?

    ....Yes.........No.............Don't know.

15. Does the teacher provide verbal instructions with visual prompts (e.g., writing on the chalkboard etc.)?

    ....Yes.........No.............Don't know.

16. Does the teacher offer accommodations for students with learning disabilities or attention problems?

............Yes.........No.............Don't know.

Content of homework assignments:

17. Do assignments overlap with lessons from the day but provide interest or application rather than just repetition?

............Yes.........No.............Don't know.

18. Does the teacher talk about the purpose of an assignments (e.g., practice etc)?

............Yes.........No.............Don't know.

19. Does the teacher communicate with the parents about what is being taught and explain how we can help?

............Yes.........No.............Don't know.

20. Are assignment prioritized so the parents know which ones to complete if there is limited time?

............Yes.........No.............Don't know.

21. Are some assignments voluntary?

............Yes.........No.............Don't know.

22. Does the teacher allow adaptations for difficulties with handwriting such as the use of a computer?

............Yes.........No.............Don't know.

23. Are some assignments active (e.g., gathering resources, interviewing others, collecting, observing natural phenomena)?

............Yes.........No.............Don't know.

Collecting, grading and returning assignments:

24. Has the teacher provided students with a system to track homework assignments?

............Yes.........No.............Don't know.

25. Are rewards for completing homework as great as the consequences for not completing homework?

............Yes.........No.............Don't know.

26. Do students turn in an excuse sheet when as assignment is misread?

    ....Yes..........No.............Don't know.

27. Does the teacher allow a certain number of excused homework assignments?

Tips to communicate effectively with child's teachers

One of the most important roles for homework is to form a connection between our family and our child's teachers. When a new school year starts, we must attend back to school to meet teachers. This is an opportunity to obtain an overview of how the teacher manages the class and what will be expected of our child. Listen carefully and ask questions. Use this meeting as an opportunity to understand how and when homework will be assigned, what it will involve and how we can best communicate with our child's teachers.

We cannot emphasize too strongly the importance of clear, timely communication in regard to homework. If our child has a history of struggling with learning or homework, it is suggested that we should request a brief meeting with our child's teachers, specifically to discuss homework. In addition to phone calls and e-mails, face-to-face meetings, though occurring less frequently, may be most effective means of developing an efficient communication system. It is critical that these brief meetings are initiated early in the school year. When meetings are held be punctual and respect the teacher's time limits. Keep in mind the following guidelines:

- Be prepared. Bring samples of the child's homework we (parents) would like to discuss. Begin the meeting with a positive comment.
- Be a good listener. Make sure we understand what is being said and the notes.
- Be honest. If we are struggling, say so. Do not blame anyone for homework problems. Focus on process and solutions.
- Ask questions and accept suggestions. Keep in mind that everyone wants what is best for the child.

In some situations a daily home note can be an effective means of communication concerning homework between school and home. Daily home notes, sometimes referred to, as daily report cards can be effective for students experiencing homework problems. Such home notes provide an opportunity for parents to communicate with teachers, and more closely monitor their child's daily school progress. Home notes can vary in detail. Most teachers maintain a file of different types of notes that can be used for specific problems. Home notes can be easily modified to meet each child's needs.

Although such notes can be quiet helpful, they can also at times be harmful to the child. Nothing is more demanding to a child struggling in school than to receive a negative note day after day. If a child cannot meet classroom expectations, perhaps a new goal needs to be set that is more inline with the child's immediate ability. We cannot over-emphasize the importance of communication between parents and teachers about student progress. If our child is struggling with homework, there is a good chance our child is also struggling with class work. It is our role as a parent to understand why our child may be having problems and what the school and we together can do to help.

Essential homework skills:

Skill One: *Starting assignments effectively*: Difficulty in beginning an assignment efficiently is a common problem for many children. It is suggested that assist the child by first identifying the primary source of the problem. Does this problem result from our child's inability to choose which task to begin first, an aversion or dislike of the task, an inability to ask for help, lack of a consistent getting-started routine, or difficulty knowing how to break a large task into smaller parts?

We need to help our child decides which tasks he or she can complete independently and which ones require help. It is suggested that first have the child first work on those assignments or parts of assignments he or she can complete independently and successfully. This will establish a pattern of good feelings and success. Help the child decide the order of tasks. This may be done by:

- Starting with the easiest or the most challenging tasks.
- Starting with assignments that require out of home resources such as the library.
- Starting with assignments that appear enjoyable.
- Doing parts of assignments and finishing or checking them at a later time.

For assignments requiring help, it is suggested that we should encourage our child to first attempt to complete the assignment independently. However, if he or she cannot, encourage the child to ask for help. Review a list of people our child can use a resource (e.g., parents, siblings, friends, classmates) or sources to consult (e.g., dictionary, encyclopedia, and internet). It is suggested to encourage younger children to learn to seek help that is especially important as the demands of school increase. A method is suggested with five questions or five steps:

- What is my question? Where exactly am I stuck?
- Who will I ask or call?
- What can I do before I ask or call?
- How have I gotten help for this type of problem in the past?
- Can my parents help me with this problem?

Skill Two: *Checking work for accuracy and thoroughness.*

Before homework is seen as a task that must be completed before children are granted freedom to engage in tasks of their choosing, most children rush through their homework. Therefore, it is important to help the child to develop the habit of checking its own work. In an effort to reduce boredom, it is suggested that the child moves on to another assignment and then return at a later point to check previous assignments. It is also time efficient for the child to make checklists with items he or she can cross off to make certain that essential steps for an assignment are completed. Checklist can be constructed for all kinds of assignments. A sample story-writing checklist appears as below:

STORY	WRITING	CHECKLIST
Yes	No	Name and date?
,,	,,	Main points as topic sentences?
,,	,,	Summary sections?
,,	,,	Conclusion section?
,,	,,	Spelling on the computer?
,,	,,	References on the computer?

As a way of motivating the development of a self-checking habit, it is suggested to offer incentives for homework completed with few errors. Incentives will not work, however, if the child's errors are the result of lack of understanding. In these situations either the work must be simplified or time must be spent helping the child to develop the skills necessary to complete the homework accurately.

4.2 HOMEWORK AND TEACHERS

Homework is one aspect of the general education curriculum that has been widely recognized as important to academic success. Teachers have long used homework to provide additional learning time, strengthen study and organizational skills and in some respects; keep parents informed of their children's progress. At the same time, it is a hard fact that homework is one of the biggest challenges and concerns that most of the teachers continue to face even after many years of teaching. The challenges of homework facing teachers today are all the more troublesome given the importance of meaningful and appropriate assignments. Students' achievement rises significantly when teachers regularly assign homework and students conscientiously do it, and the academic benefits increase as students move into the upper grades. "Teachers should devote energy to creating homework that is stimulating and provocative rather than banal", Howard Gardner, John H. and Elisabeth A. Hobbs Professor in Cognition and Education at the Harvard Graduate School of Education and the creator of the theory of multiple intelligences told Education World. And parents or mentors should go shoulder to shoulder with youngsters, helping to motivate them, thinking of ways in which to help them without giving the answer, and being aware of the child's special gifts and weaknesses.

Teachers should show students that they should take homework seriously. If homework is not completed, consequences need to be attached to this, such as making students complete homework during breaks, giving them a negative mark in a behaviour log, withdrawing privileges etc.

Using real-life experience and materials helps students to remember what they have learnt at school. The teachers should make homework more relevant to students by connecting what they have learnt in the classroom to their everyday life. They should ask them, for example, to use TV guides to help them learn the time by looking at when their favourite programmes are on; to measure their room and estimate how much paint would be needed to decorate it and how much that would cost; or to interview relatives as part of research into local history.

Prepare new topic by asking students to bring in material they have collected, such as leaves of different types for a biology lesson. Researching something on the Internet can also be both useful and enjoyable, although in-school access needs to be provided for students who do not have an Internet link at home.

Before we talk about guidelines, methods or responsibility, let us discuss what the researchers say about homework.

What researchers say?

Several researchers indicate the key to success for teachers is what one assigns, what one does with the assignments and what guidance one gives parents in assisting their children (Paulu, 2000; Berkowitz, 1996; Butler, 2000; Brown, 2000).

The following lists several suggestions for having success with homework:

- Assign a reasonable amount of homework. Studies suggest elementary students should have brief and understanding work. Junior high students should have no more than (1-2) hours a night. High school course load depends on what level of course work is chosen by the student (Cooper, H., 1994).

- If students are given a choice, they need to respond better. Cooper (1994) recommends the inclusion of both required and voluntary homework, with most not being graded for more than completion.
- District/school-wise policies should exist for the assignment of homework (Butler, 2000; Cooper, 1994).
- Homework should be clear in order for the students to complete it on their own (Butler, 2000).
- Homework should be linked with what the students are doing in class and should be returned with constructive comments or corrected together in class (Butler, 2000; Travers, 1998).
- Teachers should make their policies clear for students and parents, including what will be accepted, when it will be accepted and how the students should turn it in (Butler, 2000; Brown, 2000; Travers, 1998).
- Teachers should avoid using homework as a punishment ("Do this because you behaved badly") and/or as a reward ("no homework passes"). This tends to devalue its purpose (Travers, 1998).

Keeping above mentioned facts on behalf of the teachers about homework assignments, the following simple guidelines can help maximize the benefit students receive from the homework policies and practices the teachers set:

Assigning homework regularly and consistently

It is easier to get students in the habit of doing homework when schools and teachers establish a pattern. To establish a pattern the teachers must assign homework regularly and consistently.

Making sure students understand the purpose

Most students appreciate understanding the purpose of assignment, but the purpose may not become evident until students are part way through an assignment or have completed it together. The teacher must talk together with the kids about why homework as assignment is important. From the beginning, kids must know what the teacher is after. There must not be any confusion in the classroom — or little confusion — over the value of an assignment. Teacher must explain when he/she assigns the assignment.

Making assignment focused and clear

Focused assignments are easier for students to understand and complete. The homework that tries to introduce or reinforce too many ideas is less likely to contribute to learning. This is particularly true for students whose abstract thinking has not developed to the point where they can integrate many concepts successfully. Providing a focus and the necessary back ground information is critical to having class discussion of assigned readings succeed.

Assigning an appropriate amount of homework

Many educators believe that homework is the most effective for children in first through grades when it does not exceed twenty minutes each school day. From fourth through sixth grades, many educators recommend from twenty to forty minutes a school day for most students. For students in seventh through ninth grades, generally, up to two hours a school day is suitable. Ninety minutes to two and a half hours per night are appropriate for grades ten through twelve. Amounts that vary from these guidelines is fine for some students.

A common mistake, particularly among beginning teachers is to assign too much homework. It can be hard to resist doing so if parents push for more homework and assume that the best teachers assign the most homework. Most often, however, a mathematics teacher can tell after checking five algebraic equations whether students have mastered the necessary concepts.

Homework should not be overburdening. If there is too much, it becomes drudgery. We need to keep students' attention — keep them inspired and wanting to do the homework. Otherwise, it is no good.

Teachers also need to coordinate their homework assignments with those of other teachers so that students are not getting four assignments on a Tuesday night, but, no assignments on Wednesday night. This coordination most often requires leadership and support from the principal or other administrator.

Finally, teachers need to keep alert to how long students take to complete assignments. It is natural in a class full of varied students for some to take longer than others. Moreover, it is fine that some students do take longer, since research shows that students with low test scores who spent substantial time on how homework get grades as good as students with more ability who spend less time.

Using school and community resources

Teachers should try to make use of school and community resources maximum to make the homework assignment purposeful and meaningful. They should not forget that before assigning any homework, an extensive spadework is required, as homework should not be assigned just for the sake of assigning it.

Matching assignments to your (Teacher) style of teaching

Assignments are more apt to succeed if the teacher is comfortable with them.

Communicating Homework policy

The teachers should state their homework policy in advance and accordingly students may be informed in advance. The teachers should also send this homework policy home for parents to read, sign and return to school.

- All the works assign to you (students) is important to your (students') understanding of the material, and I (teacher) expect you will have attempted the homework assignments before the beginning of the class. We may use information in class that you will have discovered by doing the homework, so if you haven't done it, you will be at a disadvantage.

- The homework will be challenging, so don't expect to be able to do it in an hour the night before it is done. You will need to start working on it as soon as it is assigned, and it may take several days of thinking about it and coming back to it before it makes sense. This is a natural part of working on hard problems; don't give up! Many students give up if they don't know how to do a problem immediately. Don't do this! One of the things we are practicing is how to work through hard problems.

Introducing homework planners

Students can be asked to maintain a homework planner. A homework planner is a form of small calendar, in which students note down what homework they need to do and the deadline for completion. The teachers initially need to teach students how to use the planner, but once taught it will help them develop independent learning and organizational skills and good study habits. Homework planner might be a great help as it might increase family communication around homework and result in improved completion rate.

Providing choices

Students may all be expected to master the same material, but, they can do so in different ways. Providing choices increases the chances that students will enjoy more assignments. It also helps students feel that they control parts of their learning, which enables some to enjoy an assignment more than they would otherwise.

Building in flexibility

It is important to establish clear expectations for homework assignments, but rules such as not assigning homework on weekends or holidays can prove overly restrictive. These are often the perfect time for in-depth projects or to work with parents or peers.

Making it count

If students do not do their homework, they cannot reap its many benefits. Unfortunately, if students know they will get the same grade whether or not they turn in their homework, many won't do it.

Making homework varied

Try to avoid assigning the same kinds of homework every night. Students get bored if all assignments are similar in nature. Try mixing approaches and styles. Since it is almost impossible for all assignments to interest to all students, this approach increases the chances that all students will have some homework that they enjoy.

Short-term assignments can help students review and practice material that has already been covered in class. Long-term projects give students a chance to vary the pace of their work, delve into subjects that interest them, integrate large amounts of information, and learn to manage their time and meet deadlines.

Giving help as needed

Students who do not understand an assignment need to know that help is available from the teacher or other appropriate person. Students at risk of academic failure or with personal difficulties may need extra support with both academic and logistical aspects of homework. It is important that they know it is okay to ask for help. In fact, it is imperative that they do so.

Teachers schedule time for students in a variety of ways. Some work with them before school. Some do so during free periods or part of the lunch period. Some give out their home phone numbers.

Teachers may accept calls at home (not beyond 10.00 p.m.) from their students. Students who are embarrassed to call may do so anonymously. Most often, he or she talks through the problem with them to discover that they have missed some concepts.

- Some kids come from families who give them no time to do anything at home except chores and baby-sitting younger siblings. The teachers may ask these students to come in early in the morning or during their lunch periods to complete their homework in the classroom.
- Homework hotlines should be established (if there is none).
- "Study buddy" plan should be introduced.
- "Peer support" system may help students wade through tough assignments. The teacher can ask their students to keep handy the telephone numbers of five students whom they can call to talk over homework problems.
- Sometimes teachers can be a big help simply by alerting students to the repercussions for not doing an assignment.

Introducing organizational skill

It is effective for the teachers to provide classroom instruction on the organizational skills and then talk with parents about how best to support the application of skills at home.

Creating assignments that challenge students to think and to integrate

Homework can give students an opportunity to apply a concept beyond the controlled conditions of the classroom. It can also help students pull together and connect information from different places, sources and subjects. Good assignments often challenge students to break free of their usual way of thinking. Such assignments might require students to combine two ideas that are usually not associated.

The teachers should provide creative homework assignments. If students are not assigned with creative homework (or homework which demands creativity on the parts of students) may in the long run avoid using deep-level cognitive processing strategies, such as trying different ways to solve a problem.

Finding the appropriate level of difficulty

Research suggests that homework assignments should be designed so students can be expected to complete most of the task successfully. Teachers can accommodate varied ability levels by making some assignments optional and by allowing students to choose among several options.

Giving homework that makes learning personal

The assignments that work best have to do with the students — the assignments are personal to them. These assignments allow students to draw upon their family, cultural and community experiences and learn to appreciate better both their own and their classmates' backgrounds.

Few, if any, projects that a teacher assigns to social studies students should pack as much punch as one involving heritage. The teacher should want his or her students to learn how immediate families and communities can affect what we know, belief and so on. The teacher can ask his or her students to interview their parents to find out what three things they most wanted their children to know about life and why.

The results of this assignment will be beautiful. It will give parents and kids a time to get together and talk. Some parents can compose letters to their children describing what they value most — things like believing in oneself, dong one's best, having close family relationships, getting along with others, protecting the environment and believing in God.

Tying assignments to the present: Students often complain that they can't relate to assignment involving events that took place in the distant past. Thus, there is need to tie the assignments to the present.

Matching assignments to the skills, interest and needs of students

Students are more apt to complete homework successfully when assignments:

- Are neither too easy nor too hard.
- Match a child's preferred learning style; and
- Allow students to work on material that they truly enjoy.

Teachers with many students cannot be expected to customize all homework assignments for each student. However, most teachers can provide assignments to a heterogeneous class of students that vary in style, format and content. This assures that all students have some that suits and interests them.

It is important to provide at-risk students with homework that challenges them to work to their full potential. A student may be at-risk because of a variety of factors other than academic ability; for instance, a student may be at-risk because of Limited-English proficiency, poverty, race, geographic locations or economic disadvantages.

An at-risk student could also be in an advanced placement class or a class for gifted and talented students. Most teachers, however, gives students in their advanced placement classes assignments that differ from those in non-advanced placement classes.

Assigning cooperative homework

Teachers should try to make homework a cooperative homework instead of solitary activity. Cooperative homework may provide wonderful opportunity to students to learn and develop many necessary social skills to work cooperatively.

Teachers must ask themselves questions like what purposes does homework achieve? How do we make homework effective? Am I really interested in hearing different philosophies about the purposes of giving homework?

Encouraging and teaching good study habits

Children need good study habits in order to complete assignments successfully and gain the most from them academically. Unfortunately, many students haven't developed these skills, even by secondary school.

Schools should provide comprehensive programmes that spell out what study skills students in kindergarten through twelfth grade are expected to learn each year. This can help to assure that important skills are introduced early and nurtured throughout a students' year in school.

Kindergarten or first grade is not too early to introduce students to bringing homework home, completing it, and returning it to school. Early assignments need to be simple. For instance, very young students might be asked to bring a book for an adult to read to them — or for the child to read to an adult if he or she can do so. The adult might be asked to initial bookmark indicating that the book has been read. These early assignments help students grasp the importance of learning at home and show adults that their support for homework is critical.

Older elementary school students are ready to learn more advanced study skills. These include:

- Setting a regular time to study that fits in with the student's family schedule.
- Removing distractions (turning off the television and discouraging social phone-calls during the homework time).
- Gathering necessary supplies.
- Recording assignments in an assignment book or on a calendar.
- Note-taking.
- Managing time; and
- Organizing for a test.

Students need to review these study skill in secondary school and senior secondary school as their schedules become more complicated. It is generally observed that not all seventh-grade students are well organized. Some do not know how to handle having assignments from different teachers, or remember what they have to do and the books they need. So there is need to spend lots of time on study skills.

Reinforcing secondary school students' study skills can also reduce cramming — the biggest problems for kids at this stage.

Many students need to sharpen their study skills further as they move into senior secondary and find more demands being placed on their time. Many have trouble pacing themselves as they take on more extra-curricular activities and other social and family engagements.

There is need to encourage the students to pace themselves by collecting a block of homework assignments at the same time. For example, he or she may make several assignments on one day, all of which are due twelve days later. Students quickly learn that the assignments must be completed in order to perform satisfactorily on tests given at the end of twelve days — and that if they wait until the last minute to begin all of the assignments that their homework grades and test scores will suffer.

Students often imitate the organizing habits of important adults in their lives. Therefore, teachers can set an example by being organized themselves. They can let students know that they, too, keep calendars to avoid forgetting things. And they can comment to students as they write down on their own calendar.

Giving praise and motivate

Adults and children alike respond to praise. "You have done a great job" can go a long way toward motivating students to complete assignments. Praise must be genuine. Children recognise insincere compliments. Competitions help motivate students. Teachers should seek local and national contests for individual students or the entire class to enter. The competition will motivate the students to write because they know they will have an audience other than the teacher and their own classmates.

Providing constructive feedback

Research shows that students who received personal targeted feedback about their homework errors out performed students who received only marks/grades on their assignments. Students are more apt to complete assignments and advance their learning when they get consistent and constructive feedback. Students need to know where they excelled and where they need more work on an assignment. This conveys the vital message that homework helps students learn and is important.

Teachers can evaluate and review homework in a variety of ways. Many teachers give letter grades, others assign numbers and many provide written comments. Grading homework may motivates many students to do their best work and to learn more, but, in some situations grades may not be beneficial. For instance, written comments may be more constructive for a second grade student whose homework assignment required him or her to write a poem.

Feedback is the most helpful when teachers provide specific suggestions on how the homework can be improved and discussed problems and remedies with individual students or the whole class. Mathematics teachers may review a completed problem and point out any step in which an error has been made.

Peer feedback can also be feedback. In addition to providing students with another perspective of their work, peer feedback can help students learn cooperative social skill and teach students how to evaluate their own and other's efforts.

- A teacher should not assign anything he or she does not grade and put a comment on, and students must know that which is assigned, the teacher looks at and records. So, the students know that they are doing something for a reason.
- The teacher will receive a higher return rate on homework if he or she grades for both knowledge and skill and efforts. It is advised that it makes a difference because it says to kids that making the effort has some real value that goes beyond the esoteric value of learning something. It says that when the student puts forth the effort, he or she will be rewarded in a tangible way.

Teachers should distinguish between completion and effort

Students sometimes get stuck in the course of doing their homework because they do not understand something critical. This may be due to poor instruction, lack of clarity about the assignment or daydreaming on the part of the student during an explanation. But, the result is that the homework is not complete. A reasonable and respectful policy will take these factors into account. In addition, teachers should ask students to document what they did before abandoning their homework: what approaches they tried, for example or the names of the students they phoned for help. Such a policy sends the message that perseverance and resourcefulness are important, so students should not give up at the first sign of trouble.

If students still forget or do not finish their homework?

And, of course, this will happen. One approach is to use logical consequence. A student who has been given reasonable, respectful and related homework and who still has occasional creative excused needs to experience equally creative consequences that send the message that completing homework is a requirement of being a member of the class.

Perhaps homework is the student's ticket into homeroom. No hanging out with friends or participating in morning meeting until homework is completed. If a child does not have his/her homework, he/she goes directly to a buddy teacher's classroom to complete it. Or, perhaps a child has a choice of where to complete the homework, in the classroom within earshot of the activities of the class or in the library or guidance counsellor's office.

These consequences are liable to work for the usually conscientious student. For the more frequent offender, a more careful proactive approach is warranted. This approach may be called "incremental success" and favour it over daily failure. If this approach is used successfully and having delight in the increased responsibility and sense of pride shown by the students, of course, there are ups and downs to this process for the teacher, too, but in the end, this proactive effort often yield dramatic results.

We ask a lot from children when we ask them to do homework — we ask them to follow directions, to organize their materials, to manage their time and to work independently. It is a tall order and its value lies in students experiencing success. Only then will homework be effective in improving students' sense of responsibility and accomplishment, their academic skills and their independent study habits.

Involve and Communicate with parents

Parents often need advice about how to help support their child's learning at home. Discuss the importance of setting aside a quiet place to study, reading with and to younger children, discussing homework assignments and monitoring children to make sure they complete their homework. Students' learning improves when teachers communicate on a broad range of issues. Among the most vital of these is homework.

Parents are not expected to know or teach scientific information to their children, particularly as their children get older. Parents can be enormous help, however, in creating an environment at home that allows learning to take place. Teachers can also help create situations that allow parents and educators to work together to strengthen all learning, including what takes place at home.

Connecting with some parents can be a challenge. Many parents lead exceptionally busy lives. Some do not place as high a priority on homework as do teachers. The parents themselves may be in turmoil. Not all parents can help with homework to the extent that many teachers might hope.

Teacher should realise that when parents send us their child, they are sending them the very best they have, the very best child they could produce. They really care. The vast majority, they should believe really want to help.

Teachers can do many things to improve communication:

- Contact parents early in the school year — before problems arise.
- Let them know you are available to talk about homework or any other aspect of their child's education. This information can be communicated to parents through correspondence or at parent-teacher meetings scheduled for early in the school year.
- Make a special effort to communicate with parents/ guardians who do not initiate contact with school and

teachers. Making these parents feel welcome in the school is the first step to improve communications. For example, communications can be improved by telephoning parents who do not come to parent-teacher meetings.

Bellow is ways the teachers might suggest parents to be involved. For example, they can:

- Set a regular time for homework — one that works for the child and their family. Research shows correlation between successful students and parents, who create and maintain routines.
- Pick a fairly quite study area with lots of light and supplies close by. A desk in the bedroom is nice, but for many youngsters the kitchen table or a corner of the living room works just fine.
- Remove distractions. Turn off the television and social telephone calls during the homework time.
- Provide supplies and resources such as pencils, pens, erasers, writing paper, an assignment book and dictionary etc.
- Provide aids to good organization, such as an assignment calendar, book bag and folders.
- Encourage parents to check with the teacher, the school counsellor, or the principal if they cannot provide their child with the necessary supplies and resources.
- Look over the homework, but do not do the homework for them.
- Review teacher comments on homework that has been returned and discuss with their child.
- Contact the teacher if there is a homework problem or need they cannot resolve. Teachers may need to be flexible in scheduling meetings with parents to discuss homework problems in order to accommodate inflexible job schedules and other demands.

Provide parents with a list of questions to ask their child:

- What is your assignment today?
- Is the assignment clear?
- When is it due?
- Do you need special resources (e.g., a trip to the library or access to a computer)?
- Do you need special supplies (e.g., graph paper or poster board)?
- Have you started today's assignment? Finished it?
- Is it a long-term assignment (e.g., a term paper or science project)?
- For a major project, would it help to write out the steps or make a schedule?
- Would a practice test be useful?

Encourage parents to monitor television-viewing and select with their children the programmes they may watch. Inform parents that more than two to three hours of television viewing on school nights is related to lower student achievement. Moderate television viewing, especially when supervised by parents, can help children learn.

If problems with homework arise, work out a solution together with the parents and the child. The strategy will depend on what the problem is, how severe it is and the needs of the student. For instance:

- Is the homework too hard? Perhaps the child has fallen behind and will need extra help from the teacher, parent or tutor to catch up.
- Does the child need to make up a lot of work because of absences? The first step might be working out a schedule with the teacher.
- Has the child been diagnosed with a learning disability or is one suspected? If so, the child may need extra help and the teacher may need to adjust some assignments.
- Does the child need extra support, beyond what home and school can give? A mentor programme in the

community might be able to provide it, with the child being praised with an adult volunteer who can help with the youngster's special needs. Many good mentor good programmes operate in schools, universities, community organizations etc.

In resolving homework problems, make sure communication is clear. End a meeting with a parent only after you are sure that every one understands the strategy planned to ease the problem, follow up to make sure that the approach you agreed to is working.

Effective Communications:

It is found that the teachers generally encounter the following problems:

- Insufficient time and opportunity to communicate.
- Too many students on a given teacher's case load.
- Need for additional knowledge to facilitate communication (e.g., students' needs, whom to contact etc.).
- Other factors that hindered communication, such as lack of telecommunication facilities with teachers.

Teachers can use following strategies to maintain effective communication:

- Use technology to aid communication.
- Encourage students to keep assignment books.
- Provide a list of suggestions on how parents might assist with homework. For instance, ask parents to check with their children about homework daily.
- Provide parents with frequent communication about homework.
- Use written modes of communication (e.g., progress reports, notes, letters, forms etc.).
- Encourage the school administration to provide incentives for teachers to participate in face-to-face meetings (e.g., release time, compensation).

- Suggest that the school administration offer after school and/or peer tutoring sessions to give students extra help with homework.
- Share information with other teachers regarding students' strengthens and needs and necessary accommodations.

Issues for teachers:

The two main issues for teachers would seem to be:

(a) how to set appropriate assignments; and

(b) how to encourage lower-achieving students to complete their homework.

There is some evidence to suggest that the following strategies may be particularly helpful for lower achievers: parental communication and involvement; devising short, relevant tasks; homework planners/diaries and teaching students self-monitoring techniques.

Several researchers have recommended that teachers of pupils with low achievement/learning difficulties should tailor homework assignments to meet the needs of individual pupils. However, one study suggested that pupils feel there is a stigma attached to receiving different homework from their classmates. This implies that teachers need to handle the issue of differentiation with sensitivity.

The teachers must take sufficient time to teach and make the students learn the 'homework'. They should talk to students about the homework expectations and good homework habits. It is suggested that teachers apply the same "3R's" they use for choosing logical consequences — consequences should be respectful, related and reasonable — to choosing homework.

Teachers can help by:

- Exploring to students and their parents/guardians the purpose and benefits of homework.
- Ensuring students and parents/guardians are aware of the school's homework policy.
- Providing quality homework activities related to class work.

- Setting a suitable amount of relevant homework which is appropriate to the ability of each student.
- Ensuring that students are aware of what is expected of them, and how their work will be assessed.
- Giving students their homework taking into account, as far as possible, competing home obligations and co-curricular activities and homework set by other teachers.
- Marking/grading homework promptly and appropriately, maintaining homework records and providing feedback to students and parents or guardians.
- Alerting parents/guardians of any developing problems concerning their children's homework and suggesting strategies that they can use to assist their children with their homework.
- When teachers know which accommodations and adaptations are most useful, they can better identify appropriate practices to implement, thereby potentially increasing students' involvement, understanding and motivation to learn.

Some Precautional Measures

Whatever teachers do, they must not use homework as punishment. Doing so will lead to students resenting homework and they will no longer view it as a learning activity. Show students that the teachers take homework seriously by providing good feedback. Homework should be marked and returned as soon as possible. It should always be probably corrected. Uncorrected homework gives students the impression that all that matters is completing the task, no matter how. To save marking time, the teachers can let students correct each others homework.

Teachers should remember that children need time to enjoy the non-academic aspects of life. Too much homework or homework that is too difficult can take its toll on children and their families.

The so-called "drill and kill" assignments are great when practice and repetition are necessary to develop some basic skills, such as simple computation or editing. These exercises simply cannot be dropped from curriculum and if teachers do not want to use up a school day with such tasks, they can use homework to make sure the drill does not get lost.

It is better for the teacher not to waste time in finding out if the "students have done" rather than "have the students learned"?, which is real purpose of homework. In fact, when it comes to homework, the teacher never knows "who has done"?; the student, parent, brother, sister, a friend or the tutor? It is suggested that if teachers want to find out if the students have learnt, to collect homework and then, put a short two-three question quiz on the homework. This will determine who has really learnt and who has merely 'done'. It is also suggested that this procedure should be explained to students and parents and that teachers should neither apologize nor feel guilty.

A teacher must set the standard for diligence and accuracy. If no standard is taught to the students early in the school year in regards to effort, neatness, and accuracy, then the teacher, by accepting any work, has now taught the students, "you can turn in any kind of work you feel like and I will accept it".

Diligence and accuracy might be taught as structured lessons with models of "This is acceptable" and "This is not". Student work can be returned and done over until "they get it right" as part of a teacher's rules and routines package taught the first three weeks of school. The "acceptable model" can be reviewed throughout the school year and followed through with each time a student does not meet the standard. In terms of fairness and, if explained honestly to the class, adjustments and modifications can be made to the model to meet individual needs and abilities.

Teacher should make sure students see the relevance of homework:

Teachers should:

- Integrate it clearly into the lesson or the topic they are studying, for instance by reviewing homework at the start of the lesson.

- Make it challenging, but make sure students will be able to complete it successfully.
- Do not set task which could be confusing or frustrating.
- Do not set task which demands mere repetition.
- Consider individualising homework when teaching a set of students of mixed ability.

Do not assign homework as a punishment

Homework assignment must not be used as a punishment. Also, the teachers should make it sure that they also never use homework to complete what they could not finish during class or to introduce students to new or complicated subject matter.

As teachers develop their own philosophy about homework, consider following ideas:

- Do not give homework as punishment.
- Do not give spur-of-the-moment homework assignments, especially if you expect students to devote their time and care to the work.
- Do not assume because no questions are asked when you give the assignment that students have no questions about their homework.
- Understand that not all kinds of homework assignments are equally valuable for all students.
- Acknowledge the purpose of every assignment.
- Include parents by making your homework expectations clear and encouraging students to ask their parents for appropriate help with homework.
- Offer to help students before and after school with homework. You are the best judge about which assignments really must be completed independently.
- Do not confuse excuses for incomplete homework assignments with legitimate reasons.
- Make every effort to acknowledge completed homework assignments and if you grade/mark them, grade/mark and return them right away with feedbacks.

Justification of assignments:

As teachers, they must be able to justify the homework they have assigned. If students ask, why do I have to do this?, teachers should be able to respond right away and precisely. If they cannot justify the homework and show how it fits in the curriculum, why bother giving the assignment?

Use of Time:

Based on the literature and research regarding the use of time, there is a very strong positive relationship between academic learning time and both student achievement and attitudes. Academic learning time is the time the learner is engaged in an academic task that he/she can perform with high success. Therefore, teachers should consider the following with regard to homework: (1) matching the instruction to the students' abilities and (2) providing specific feedback to students.

Teachers have traditionally assigned homework as a way to expand their instructional time, but if it is not matched to the students' and the teacher does not have the time to give the proper feedback, then the opportunity to provide effective homework activities is significantly limited.

Additionally, the time it takes to assign, collect and correct homework, which is not designed to positively affect learning, subtracts from opportunities to plan and implement more effective classroom instruction.

Homework policy for teachers

- All students in a class will be responsible for same assignments, with only rare exception.
- Homework will include mandatory assignments. Failure to turn in mandatory assignments will necessitate remedial activities.
- Homework also will include voluntary assignment to meet the need of individual students or group of students.
- All homework assignments will not be formally evaluated. They will be used to locate problems in student progress and to individualize instruction.

- Topics will appear in assignments before and after they are covered in class, not just on the day they are discussed.
- Homework will not be used to teach complex skills. It will generally focus on simple skills and material or on the integration of skills already possessed by the student.
- Parents will rarely be asked to play a formal instructional role in homework. Instead, they should be asked to create a home environment that facilitates student self-study.

Teachers should:

- Be familiar with the homework policy (if any).
- Develop individual practices that are consisted with the homework policy (if any).
- Make assignments meaningful to the students and relevant to the lesson.
- Develop criteria by which homework is to be evaluated.
- Insure purpose and directions are clear and concise to promote student understanding.
- Make certain the students have the proper skill and materials to complete assignments.
- Make it sure that the students have multiple ways to complete their homework with the resources available to them.
- Develop and communicate a make-up policy to students.
- Provide a means for notifying parents of homework quality and completeness.
- To avoid homework overload, communicate with students and/or teachers concerning other assignments. A well integrated co-ordination is required on the part of teachers themselves (different discipline) and parents.
- Flexible assignments are important, because each one's ability is diverse. Also, we have students who have access to all resources; we have some students who have nothing.

- Insure that the students have been taught the skills and information necessary to complete the assignment.
- Determine that the students clearly understand what is completed.
- Establish assignments consistent with the maturity and ability of the students.
- Encourage students to realize the regular study, as well as written work, is an integral part of homework.
- Consider the cost and availability of necessary materials, especially if many students need to use the same materials or equipment.
- Give adequate time for completion of assignments and long-term assignments consider periodic progress check.
- Use directions when routine assignments are made for completion over weekends or holidays.
- Evaluate and/or review all homework, written or otherwise, in a timely and appropriate manner.
- Use assignments to evaluate instruction and/or students progress.
- Provide long-term, short-term and independent assignments to encourage students to use study time wisely, efficiently and effectively.
- Consider that students have other academic, cultural and social commitments that are of benefit to them.
- Contact the parent when the student repeatedly fails to complete homework.

Show respect for students

Students are more inclined to complete assignments when teachers and students respect one another. Students sense when teachers care about them and want them to do their best work. Every teacher must talk to his or her kids. Teachers should be closed to their students. They should know them personally. Kids will do things for the teachers if they know that teachers respect them as people, as real people and not just as students — that you care about them as human beings.

Teachers must know every student personally by name. This is very important. As a result of this, kids will do more homework. Half the reason they do the homework is because they likes their teachers. It is not always because they realise 'it is' in their best interest.

If the students know how the teacher really cares about how they do, if they know that the teacher likes and cares about them, they are going to try harder. Toward that end, the teacher should talk privately with any student who is not doing well — and who is not completing homework assignments. "Screaming and yelling do not work." There is need to reason out, to tell them why it is important to do well. Teachers need to convince the students that their family really wants them to do well. If they want to support their family and have nice lifestyle, they need a good job with benefits. For all those things they all need an education. Education is the key that unlocks the shackles of poverty.

The teacher can tell the students that they can negotiate to change when an assignment is due if something major intervenes — for example, a major sporting event in which they want to participate or a major social or family function in which they want to participate. The teacher should sometimes challenge why they cannot get the assignments done. But, the fact that the students must know that the teacher is willing to take their needs into consideration sets a tone of respect that reverberate throughout his or her classroom.

Students sense when teachers are committed to their learning and view it as valuable for both students and teachers alike.

Teachers should sometimes adopt such methods that can encourage the students to criticize even teachers' work. This will help them see learning as a two-way processes. They should see that it is worthwhile to do the work and get feedback from others. The more able students see that the assignment is not just busy work. Teachers are a vital link in making this happens.

Teachers' Responsibility

Teachers have a responsibility when assigning homework to "let kids know what you are teaching through the homework and why." But, it is found that in perspective education or in professional development there is no such training. There is need to have such input in our professional courses which are for the preparation of prospective teachers.

Teachers are responsible for:

- Informing students and parents of their classroom homework policies and proceed.
- Identifying the degree to which the assessment of homework affects student's grade.
- Selecting and assigning homework, which meets the criteria, outlined above.
- Monitoring the students as they record the assignments in the planner.
- Providing sufficient classroom instruction, clear and complete directions modalities.
- Checking homework for completeness and mastery of concepts and skills as appropriate to the assignment.
- Informing students and parents of student performance and completion of homework assignments as appropriate.

Teachers need to consider how parents can contribute to a child's development:

- Make homework assignments useful. Children need ways to practice their new learning in the home setting. They do not need busy work.
- Send home required texts. It makes it very difficult for parents to help their child when they do not have access to the information.
- Provide all materials needed for the assignments. As far as possible, do not expect parents to purchase or locate materials.

- Offer ways for parents to check on homework after hours. Also, provide a way for families to get help with homework.
- Establish consistent routines for students to use in bringing homework home and returning it. Teach the homework routine to the children and inform families of it.
- Send home assistive technology devices used at school. Tell families about strategies and accommodations that work in the classroom.
- Share resources for helping children with homework (e.g., tutoring, after school homework programme).

Design and communicate homework assignments that meet appropriate learning objectives such as:

- Review of key instruction taught in class.
- Practice and/or reinforcement of new skills.
- Preparation for a new lesson.
- Application or synthesis of skills learnt.
- Preparation for tests.
- An assessment of students' understanding.
- Provide homework expectations at beginning of school year.
- Explain how homework is rated.
- Clearly explain assignments orally and in writing.
- Use a consistent method of posting and explaining assignments so students record their accurately.
- Monitor the time used by the students to complete assignments and adjust as needed.
- Assess homework in a timely and informative manner so that students benefit from the feedback.
- Clearly identify the consequences for incomplete, missing, late and substandard homework.

- Inform students and parents when homework is repeatedly incomplete, late, missing and substandard homework.
- Inform the students and parents of the system for obtaining missed homework.
- Make efforts to coordinate the completion of long-term projects, tests etc. with team and special area teachers.
- Guide students in the development of skill.
- To instruct students in the use of skills such as outlining, graphic organizers and reading for understanding.
- To guide in how to brake long stream assignments into smaller steps.

Some tips

- Planning and setting homework is the responsibility of the teachers in each group.
- Announce assignments properly.
- Inform students of the purpose of the assignment.
- Show relevancy.
- Written instructions on board or on assignments sheet help.
- Create assignments that arouse curiosity, stimulate thinking, provide good practice, opportunities and/or application of knowledge.
- Consider using study guides, puzzles, or other accountability measures when assigning reading.
- Coordinate assignments to eliminate too many assignments at a time.
- Set up weekly assignment and assessment calendars to facilitate coordination.
- Assign appropriate time for each assignment depending on its complexity and length while considering the availability to all students of special resources needed (i.e. computers).

- Schedule long-term assignments given by the team throughout the school year to eliminate overburdening student schedules. Each long-term assignment will be given in writing with intermediate due dated to train the student in long-term planning.
- List assignments in the classroom in a standard location and give them orally for students to put in their assignment notebook given an approximate time needed for completion.
- Provide time for homework help (before or after school, in study time or during activity/team periods).
- Provide timely feedback for assignments.
- Distribute a written homework guideline to every student at the beginning of each course.

Questions and Concerns

"What about the children who never do their homework?" (I have tried just about everything and nothing helps.)

"What about the students who only do part of the assignments?"

"What about the kids who don't do it because there is no one around at home to help them?"

If we are like most teachers, we have probably experienced all of these problems and more. Is it possible to make them all disappearing? Unlikely, but, it is possible to greatly reduce the number of problems and to increase the chances that all students will experience success.

Few suggestions : The typical approach to introducing homework is to talk with students about homework expectations. We tell them how they are to do their homework; we may even talk about good homework habits. We then send them off to do it alone, and more often than not, we are disappointed with the results.

The critical help that is missing here is practice. If we really want students to understand our expectations for homework and successfully meet these expectations, then we must be willing to "teach" homework. This means introducing homework slowly and incrementally and providing plenty of time for students to practice the routine under our guidance before expecting them to do it at home independently.

For example, during the first few weeks of school, primary grade students can be asked to complete all written homework in class. Older students can be asked to do the same for the first two to four weeks. During this practice period, teachers and students can work to define expectations for high-quality homework and students bring home their completed homework to share with parents. In this way, parents gain a better understanding of homework expectations and are better able to hold their children to these expectations.

- It is never too late to begin.
- Be flexible and individualized as needed.
- Involve parents extensively but judiciously.

It is often the case that all students are given identical homework assignments. This practice guarantees failure for some students. Discouraged by their inability to meet expectations, many students invent ingenious excuses. Their willingness to invent energy creating excuses, however, is a sign of their continued eagerness to do what is expected of them.

If we are to increase students' success with homework, we must be willing to be flexible and to individualize assignments. Differentiated homework, like differentiated instruction, will be more work for the teacher in the short run, but the long-term pay-off of student success and investment will be worth it.

It is suggested that teachers should apply the same "3R's" they use for choosing logical consequences — consequences should be responsible, related and reasonable — to choosing homework. That is homework should be:

- Respectful of the child's ability and developmental level,
- Related to the work of the classroom and, where possible, to the interest of the individual student, and
- Reasonable in amount and degree of difficulty.

This does not mean that teachers need to create different homework assignment for every student every day, of course. There are obviously some assignment that every one has to do and can easily accomplish.

Specific differentiation is needed, however, for those students whose ability or work ethic is in need of support. There may be a student, who struggles with mathematics. Anticipating this, the teacher might adjust the length of the assignment accordingly.

Other modifications might include arranging for a child, to get help with a homework assignment from a parent or sibling or modifying the way in which an assignment is done.

The important question to ask is, "How might I modify this assignment to fit the child's learning style and needs?" By having students complete homework assignments in school during the early weeks of school, teachers can learn a lot about students' varying abilities to work independently, information which can be sued to adjust expectations accordingly.

The most important strategy for involving parents is to inform them of our homework practices. Clearly the more informed parents are about homework expectations; the better able they will be to help their children meet these expectations. Teachers and schools should send a letter to parents at the beginning of the school year explaining the homework policy and expectations and enlisting parent support.

A great early-in-the-year class project could be to write our own "homework manual" as a class, perhaps with a "homework hint" from each student and send the manual home to parents. Having students completed their first homework assignments at school and bringing them home to share with their family will also help parents gain a clear understanding of homework expectations.

Guidelines for teachers

At the secondary school level, the teacher has autonomy to assign homework to their students based on what they believe will best assist the students in their educational programme.

The wide range of courses offered, the various levels of courses, and the diversified curricula are the reasons for this autonomy.

There are, however, certain procedures that all teachers, regardless of curriculum area are expected to adhere to concerning homework. These include the following items:

(A) Each teacher should distribute to every student a written homework guideline at the beginning of each course. This guideline is to be required by the student and parent, signed and returned to the teacher. The teachers' guideline includes, but is not limited to, the following information:

- A description of the various types of homework assignments a student might expect during the course.
- The teacher should provide the date each assignment is due.
- The method in which assignments will be given to the students.
- The average amount of time a student might need to complete the different types of assignments.
- The procedure for turning in assignments late, including any penalty.
- The grading weight and expected length of various written assignments.
- The expected format of the assignment e.g., medium of use, material, bibliography required, etc.

(B) The homework guidelines will be shared with parents at meet the teachers programme.

(C) Teachers should review the homework guidelines. Also, they should try to get feedback from different resources and persons concerned.

(D) Long-term assignments need to be communicated, as far as possible, to the students and parents in advance.

Some other relevant guidelines:

- Homework should be assigned with specific instructional purposes and related to the classroom activities, themes, objectives etc.

- All teachers of a particular class (i.e. regular classroom teacher, special education teacher, music teachers, physical education teacher etc.) should coordinate.
- Homework tasks should be appropriate to students' levels of achievement and individual differences inability must be considered. Expectations for homework tasks must then be adapted accordingly.
- Teachers should be cognizant of factors such as co-curricular activities home/family support and children's interest in assigning tasks.
- All tasks should be explained clearly keeping in mind the varying ability levels of children within a class. Whenever applicable, concise written instructions would ensure parents have a clear understanding of the tasks involved.
- It is recommended that homework planners/notebooks be used to record daily homework tasks. A regular check of these planners is essential. Parental review of the planner each evening is strongly recommended.
- Homework should be collected by the teacher, graded and returned with feedbacks in a timely fashion.
- A clear statement of expectations for homework at each grade level should be included in the parent packages given at Parent Orientations. Such expectations could include, for instance:
  (a) the correcting of errors in homework tasks.
  (b) expectations for neatness.
  (c) the use of manuscript vs. cursive writing.
- When homework assignments are consistently not being completed, parental contact is essential (phone calls, notes in planners etc.). An appropriate plan of action should be developed between the student, parent and teacher. This plan should be appropriate to the child's needs and home influences.

- Time should be made each day for students to record homework tasks and prepare materials for homework assignments. When two or more teachers are involved, consistent routines for recording homework are essential. Students need to be aware of the expectations of all teachers involved.

What teachers can tell parents about homework?

- When your child does homework, you do homework, such as balancing a check book.
- When your child asks for help, provide guidance, not answers. Show your child that the skills they are learning are related to things you do as an adult. If your child is reading, you read too.
- When the teacher asks that you play a role in homework, do it. Giving answers means your child will not learn the material. To much help teaches your child that when the going gets rough, someone will do the work for him.
- If homework is meant to be done by your child alone, stay away.

If homework is meant to be done by your child what teachers can tell parents about homework?

- Stay informed about your child's good assignments.
- Help your child figure out what is hard homework and what is easy homework.
- Watch your child for signs of failure or frustration.
- Reward progress in homework.

Homework Tips for Teachers Checklist

1. Do you (teacher) provide the purpose of an assignment?
   ....Yes.........No.............Don't know.
2. Is the due date provided?
   ....Yes.........No.............Don't know.
3. Are materials necessary to successfully complete the assignment recommended?
   ....Yes.........No.............Don't know.

4. Are the requirements for good performance explained, including the steps necessary for a long-term assignment or a project?

   ....Yes..........No..............Don't know.

5. Is there a system in place for students to obtain help when needed?

   ....Yes..........No..............Don't know.

6. Do you (teacher) provide time at the end of class for students to compare their understanding of homework assignments?

   ....Yes..........No..............Don't know.

7. Do you (teacher) ask students to repeat the assignments in their own words?

   ....Yes..........No..............Don't know.

8. Do you (teacher) provide time for students to begin their assignments in class at joined desks or tables?

   ....Yes..........No..............Don't know.

9. Do you (teacher) require students to rewrite or repeat directions before beginning written assignments?

   ....Yes..........No..............Don't know.

10. Is there a system in place whereby students can ask for help if they do not understand written instructions?

    ....Yes..........No..............Don't know.

11. Are students taught a system to highlight instructions with coloured markers?

    ....Yes..........No..............Don't know.

12. Do you (teacher) provide an outline on a weekly or monthly basis of assignments and deadlines?

    ....Yes..........No..............Don't know.

13. Do you (teacher) have a system to make certain that students have assignment books, homework planners or homework buddies to call in the event of problems?

    ....Yes..........No..............Don't know.

14. Do you (teacher) offer assignments at the beginning of the class rather than at the end when students may be thinking about recess or lunch?

............Yes.........No.............Don't know.

15. Do you (teacher) provide verbal instructions with visual prompts (e.g., writing on the chalkboard etc)?

............Yes.........No.............Don't know.

16. Do you (teacher) offer accommodations for students with learning disabilities or attention problems?

............Yes.........No.............Don't know.

Content of homework assignments:

17. Do assignments overlap with lessons from the day but provide interest or application rather than just repetition?

............Yes.........No.............Don't know.

18. Do you (teacher) talk about the purpose of an assignment (e.g., practice etc)?

............Yes.........No.............Don't know.

19. Do you (teacher) communicate with parents about what is being taught and explain how we can help?

............Yes.........No.............Don't know.

20. Are assignments prioritized so that you (teacher) may suggest to students which one to complete if there is limited time?

............Yes.........No.............Don't know.

21. Do you (teacher) provide assignments voluntary?

............Yes.........No.............Don't know.

22. Do you (teacher) allow adaptations for difficulties with handwriting such as the use of a computer?

............Yes.........No.............Don't know.

23. Are some assignments provided by you (teacher) active (e.g., gathering resources, interviewing others, collecting, observing natural phenomena)?

............Yes.........No.............Don't know.

Collecting, grading/marking and returning assignments:

24. Have you (teacher) provided students with a system to track homework assignments?

    ....Yes..........No..............Don't know.

25. Are rewards for completing homework as great as the consequences for not completing homework?

    ....Yes..........No..............Don't know.

26. Do you (teacher) ask students turn in an excuse sheet when as assignment is misread?

    ....Yes..........No..............Don't know.

27. Do you (teacher) allow a certain number of excused homework assignments?

    ....Yes..........No..............Don't know.

4.3 HOMEWORK AND STUDENTS

The whole purpose of assigning the homework is to facilitate learning. By establishing a family routine of talking about the value of learning of which homework is one means of accomplishing this goal, the meaning of homework shifts from just a boring task requiring repetitive effort to a valuable system for learning. You (students) must not forget that homework activities help you to develop essential skills for independent learning. The "drill and kill" assignments, which requires to solve all the odd problems from a long list of mathematical equations, for instance, may not be liked very much, but, still such exercises are good exercise for the development of the mind.

Students can learn more and get better grades in school when they do their own homework assignments. In addition, students will benefit in many other ways from doing homework assignments. Some of the benefits are:

- They become capable.
- They learn to be self-reliant and self-directed.
- Completing homework on time builds responsibility, character and perseverance.

- It is through doing homework that students practice time management skills, taking initiative and being resourceful.
- The most serious consequence of not completing homework is lost of learning.
- Finally, homework provides the opportunity for children to take pride in their accomplishments.

Students can help by:

- Being aware of the importance of homework.
- Being aware of their school's homework policy.
- Completing homework within the given time frame.
- Alerting parents or guardian to homework expectation.
- Seeking assistance from teachers and parents or guardian when difficulties arise.
- Showing their homework to their parents or guardians.
- Ensuring homework is of a high standard.
- Organizing their time to ensure that sufficient time is given to quality homework within set deadlines.

Organizational Skills

Homework problems can be overcome with basic study skills and organizational skills. Among the organizational skills most basic to homework are:

- Identifying a location for doing homework is free of distractions.
- Having materials available and organized.
- Allocating enough time to complete activities and keeping on schedule.
- Taking good notes.
- Developing a sequential plan for completing multi-task assignments.
- Checking assignments for accuracy and completion.
- Knowing how to get help.
- Turning in completed homework on time.

Students Responsibilities

- Use the homework assignments notebook to keep a record of all assignments, tests and other responsibilities. Collect the necessary materials (books, worksheets, etc.) needed to complete the assignments.
- Ask questions and seek help without any hesitation if confused about the assignment or any part of the work.
- Be responsible for completing and returning all homework assignments on time to the teacher. Follow all expected standards of quality concerning heading, neatness, content and directions.
- Budget time wisely and share time plans with parents/ guardians, especially on long-range assignments.
- As far as possible, study in a quiet and preferred place with few interruptions and distractions that limit focus.
- Consult the homework hotline (if any).
- Participate actively and cooperatively in the evaluation of their homework when appropriate.

Students should

- Be familiar with the teacher's expectations concerning homework.
- Demonstrate a commitment to the importance of homework.
- Develop a system for remembering homework assignments.
- Complete homework assignments on time, as directed by the teacher.
- Budget time to complete homework assignment.
- Use an appropriate study environment (i.e. time, materials, space and conditions).
- Request help when needed to complete complicated homework assignments. Be responsible for making up missed assignments.
- Understand the assignment prior to leaving the classroom.

- Maintain the homework assignment notebook as directed to maximize its effectiveness in assisting with homework completion and student organization.
- Write all assignments in their school designed homework assignment notebook.
- Share the homework assignment notebook and all teacher communications with parents.
- Examine daily schedules with parental help and set aside time to do homework.
- Work with parents to create a positive study/work environment.
- Prioritize homework assignments.
- Complete long-term homework assignments in manageable steps.
- Learn from homework, rather than just rushing to finish it.
- Review class notes.
- Do your work and never plagiarize.
- Find out what work has been missed due to absence or any other reason.
- Make up missed work.
- Take pride in your homework.

Personal Responsibilities

The fulfilment of the following personal responsibilities is important if the student is to perform well at school:

- Completing assigned homework as directed and in the spirit in which it was assigned.
- Returning homework to the teacher by the designated time.
- Submitting homework assignments that reflect careful attention to detail and quality of work.
- Reading some books other than textbooks every four or five weeks.

Strategies for making up missed work

- Ask the teacher what was missed.
- Seek extra help as needed.
- Call a "homework buddy".
- Ask a classmate to collect notes and handouts.
- When a student is absent for three or more days, contact the homework-counselling centre (if there is any).
- Attend homework club (if any) with school counsellors.

To comply with each teacher's guideline

At the secondary school level, students are expected to understand the vitality of homework and are responsible to comply with each teacher's guideline. The students should:

- Read/review each teacher's guideline on homework.
- Sign them and get it signed by their parents and return it to the teacher as instructed.
- Read and follow the policy against plagiarism as stated in the code of conduct.
- Take responsibility for getting all homework assignments, whether they are in class.
- Stay after school upon request and/or when necessary to work on assignments with the teacher.
- Present a written explanation to the teacher when circumstances beyond his/her control prevent timely return of an assignment; this explanation will be signed by the parent/guardian.
- Complete assigned homework. Homework is the responsibility of the students, not the parents, siblings or other party. Homework is practice and the benefits of doing it well will be reaped at assessment times.

Use school and community resources:

Students should try to make use of school and community resources optimally to complete the homework assignment purposefully and meaningfully. They should not forget that before submitting the homework assignments, an extensive and exhaustive work is required, as homework should not be submitted just for the sake of submitting it.

Maintain homework planners

Students must maintain a homework planner. A homework planner is a form of small calendar, in which students note down what homework they need to do and the deadline for completion. The students need to learn initially how to use the planner, but once learnt it will help them develop independent learning and organizational skills and good study habits. Homework planner might be a great help as it might increase family communication around homework and result in improved completion rate.

Ask teachers to provide choices

You (student) may all be expected to master the same material, but, you (student) can do so in different ways. If you (student) have an opportunity of choices, you (student) will find the homework assignment interesting and enthralling. It will help you (student) to have a feeling that you control parts of your learning, which enables some of you to enjoy an assignment more than you would otherwise.

You (student) can ask teachers to make homework varied

Students may feel mental weariness produced by monotonous assignments. Since it is almost impossible for all assignments to interest to all students, this approach increases the chances that all students will have some homework that they enjoy. Varied homework assignments can give students a chance to vary the pace of their work, delve into subjects that interest them, integrate large amounts of information, and learn to manage your time and meet deadlines.

Ask for help as needed

Students who do not understand an assignment need to know that help is available from the teacher or other appropriate person. Students at risk of academic failure or with personal difficulties may need extra support with both academic and logistical aspects of homework. It is important that they know it is okay to ask for help. In fact, it is imperative that they do so.

Develop good study habits

Students need good study habits in order to complete assignments successfully and gain the most from them academically. Unfortunately, many students have not developed these skills, even by secondary school.

These include:

- Setting a regular time to study that fits in with the student's family schedule.
- Removing distractions (turning off the television and discouraging social phone-calls during the homework time).
- Gathering necessary supplies.
- Recording assignments in an assignments book or on a calendar.
- Note-taking.
- Managing time; and
- Organizing for a test.

Students need to review these study skill in secondary school and senior secondary school as their schedules become more complicated. It is generally observed that not all seventh-grade students are well organized. Some do not know how to handle having assignments form different teachers, or remember what they have to do and the books they need. So there is need to spend lots of time on study skills.

Many students need to sharpen their study skills further as they move into senior secondary and find more demands being placed on their time. Many have trouble pacing themselves as they take on more extra-curricular activities and other social and family engagements.

There is need to encourage the students to pace themselves by collecting a block of homework assignments at the same time. For example, he or she may make several assignments on one day, all of which are due twelve days later. Students quickly learn that the assignments must be completed in order to perform satisfactorily on tests given at the end of twelve days — and that if they wait until the last minute to begin all of the assignments that their homework grades and test scores will suffer.

Involve and Communicate with parents

Discuss the importance of setting aside a quiet place to study, reading with and to younger children, discussing homework assignments and monitoring yourself (students) to make sure you complete homework.

Bellow is ways the teachers might suggest parents to be involved. For example, they can:

- Ask your parents to check with the teacher, the school counsellor, or the principal if your parents cannot provide you with the necessary supplies and resources.
- Ask your parents to look over the homework.
- Ask your parents to review teacher comments on homework that has been returned and discuss with you.
- Ask your parents to contact the teacher if there is a homework problem or need your parents cannot resolve.

Develop a habit of mandatory homework time

Mandatory homework time means that students must use the 'entire' schedule daily homework time for homework reading. If two hours is allotted each night, then the extra time must be used reviewing, practicing or reading, without exception.

A system of returning homework to school on time

When homework is completed, students usually are able to access enjoyable activities. Thus, it is not surprising that some students view the completion of homework rather than turning the homework in as the end point in the process. You (students) may have completed homework at school or at home but misplaced it, misread the teacher's instructions to turn it in, or forget to bring the assignment to school.

It is important for the students to develop the independent habits to return homework to school. Students who forget to bring homework to school should first try keeping a homework folder in their backpack. When the homework is finished each night, develop the habit of putting the homework in the folder and in the backpack at night to be returned to school the next day. You may need to remind yourself in the morning to look over assignments due that day.

When you experience difficulty remembering to turn in assignments, you may ask the teacher to develop a system to provide a cue to you to turn homework in.

A more independent system to remind our child to remember to turn homework is to create an assignment-tracking sheet. You should develop the skill to mark assignments in each subject when they are due and whether a book, notebook, or worksheet needs to be brought home to complete the assignment.

With the increasing use of technology, homework at time can be faxed or e-mailed to school. The Internet may be used to access the teacher's online files if the school has such a system in place. This system allows you to check yours progress on a weekly basis.

Creating a time, place and plan

Homework needs to fit into the flow of the family. For some students working at the kitchen table while dinner is being prepared can be fine, and for other students having a designated place in the house to complete homework, away from family activity is the most productive. It is important to understand how you are best able to work and concentrate.

You should have some choices regarding time and place. Some students are comfortable alone in their bedroom while others will choose the kitchen table. Important criterion:

- Study in the same place everyday.
- Do work on a hard surface.
- Ask yourself...can you concentrate there?

- Supplies should be at the fingertips.
- No distractions.

Have a regular time for doing homework, but be flexible. Homework time should neither be too late in the evening nor when you are tired. Following time schedule for homework is an effective way of increasing the number of assignments completed. However, when you do not maintain the time schedule, you may discover that you are lagging behind. Therefore, it is important for you to consistently follow this schedule as a rule. You must remember that behaviour needs to be repeated many, many times before it becomes a habit or a routine.

You need to learn effectively manage your time—both your free time and homework time for school and life success.

Some tips:

- Prioritize the things — a good way to manage time.
- To make prioritize "to-do" list.
- List the activities from the time school gets out until bedtime.
- Prioritize homework assignments onto a to-do list.
- Use a calendar to keep track of dates and deadlines.
- You need to learn to record information in advance so you can plan for upcoming assignments and events.
- You need to design your own personalized calendar.

Preferably, homework should be completed immediately after a snack (or playtime) but before preferred activities (e.g., television). It is suggested that you must consider a number of short homework periods in the early afternoon interspersed with preferred activity times. A daily plan can be planned by a written or tape-recorded list of activities specifying times to be spent on homework, chores, and preferred activities. It is also suggested that you should develop a list of preferred activities. These can be available when homework is completed. Preferred activities can be as simple as additional time prior to bedtime and can be used to increase the number of minutes you spend on homework.

How to make learning time management fun

- Write the name of the month on top of twelve blank calendar pages. Put them in order in a folder, section of the notebook or on a bulletin board/wall.
- Go through each month and write the names of important events — tests, assignment dates, vacation dates, sports schedules, birthdays, party dates etc. Glue to a piece of construction paper and creatively decorate the background for each calendar to give it a "personal touch".
- Hole punch for notebook. If hanging, put holes at the top and string together with two loops of yarn. Then hang with paper clips.
- Each month, add important dates to your calendar.

Short-cut tips:

- Try colour coding events for 'at-a-glance' searching, i.e. write homework in red, tests in blue, vacation dates in green and so on.
- *Make a weekly study plan* : Use a weekly planner to remember all kinds of information. If the school has one — use it. Transfer important events from monthly calendar to weekly plan. Put all assignments and due dates in it. Frame and hang it for quick reference.
- Estimate how long assignments and activities will take. When you can estimate the time it takes to complete a job, you can make good choices as to when to start. *Only practice at estimation leads to accuracy.*
- Break down big assignments into smaller parts to make time for each part. This prevents it from becoming overwhelming and discourages waiting to the last minute.

How to help yourself to manage difficult or long-term assignments

Students struggling to manage difficult or long-term assignments will need to develop self-management skills. If you are overwhelmed by multi-steps projects or confusing assignments, your first reaction is to ask for help or put the assignment off for another time. A number of strategies can help you handle these types of assignments:

- *Underlining*. Use magic markers to highlight important parts of directions.
- Read all of the headings, table of contents, chapter questions and bolded words in reading assignments. Highlight or write them down if that helps. Highlight directions in any worksheet. If it is a mathematics sheet, highlight symbols and signs.
- Make lists of important words or concepts.
- Tell yourself brief summaries into a tape recorder. Play them back and listen carefully. Do they make sense?

It is also suggested that you review your assignments to determine if there are any long-term projects waiting to be completed. You should set up a schedule to complete the assignment in a step-by-step fashion. It is useful to focus your attention on the main feature of the task (e.g. to outline, headings, words in italics or bold, the questions at the end or the beginning of the work). Based on just these general features of complex tasks or reading material, this strategy will help children reduce large amounts of information to topics, questions or categories.

There are other ways to reduce information or to make directions easier to understand. For example, you can use magic markers to not only highlight directions but key points as well. Once you are able to identify the important points, you can use a different coloured marker to mark the supporting points. This strategy can also be used in listing to teachers' lectures. If notepaper were divided into three columns, students could take notes on the main points in column one, supporting points in column two and questions or thought in column three.

4.4 HOMEWORK AND SCHOOLS

Research tells us that time spent doing homework directly affects a child's achievement. Students who consistently do homework perform academically better than those who do not do homework. By doing homework, students can improve academic achievement in all subjects. This occurs across all grade levels or both high and low achievers.

Homework for the school-age child is an opportunity to learn the valuable organizational skill for strong study habits. Parents can get the most out of homework for their child when the school is in a commanding position to make them understand the purpose of its values it encourages.

The schools can take following steps:

1. Homework policy.
2. After-school academic sessions.
3. The homework centre.
4. The homework hotline.
5. The tutorial programme.

Homework policy: Every school must have a homework policy. It is advised that the schools must include teachers, parents and students in any effort to set homework policies. Policies should address the purposes of homework (not to be used as punishment); amount and frequency; school and teacher responsibilities (e.g., coordination of assignments, clear directions, home-school communications); student responsibilities; the role of parents or others who assist students with homework; and equity issues (accommodations for students with disabilities, availability of support and resources). [For detail see chapter-3 (Homework Policy)].

After-school academic sessions: During four of the five days of the school week, teachers work with students for one hour after the end of classes. Students may choose which teacher they wish to spend this hour with. During this time, no sports or other extra-curricular activities are allowed to take place. The school department should arrange with the transportation system to pick all students up from school one hour later than in previous years.

The homework centre: During four of the five days of the school week, students have the option to study in the

Homework Centre for an additional one and half hour following the after-school academic sessions. The Centre is located in classrooms adjacent to the exit closest to the bus pick-up area so that students may study while waiting for the bus if they wish.

The homework hotline: There should be a 24-hour Homework assignment hotline designed to accommodate all students, from the one who forgot to bring home his/her assignment book to the one who was out sick for the day. Teachers have a recording of all homework assigned that day, and in some cases, for days in advance. Teachers can also leave messages announcing upcoming tests, field trips and other special events on the hotline.

The tutorial programme: There is a need to identify students as needing individual tutoring in certain subject areas. The tutorial sessions meet during the after school academic session one or two afternoons a week and are coordinated by schoolteachers.

Outlines of strategies that schools can use to reach out to all parents and help involve them in their children's education

Schools should tell parents how they can reach them and when. Would the school prefer that they telephone? Write a note? Set up a meeting with the school? What hours should the school prefer that they call? May the parents call the teachers at certain times at home, or would the teachers prefer that they do so at school?

All students should be given a homework assignment book on the first day of school. The homework assignment book may play a central role in helping students get organized and complete assignments on time. The homework assignment book also provides an easy and efficient way for parents and teachers to communicate with one another about assignments; if either has questions or concerns, they exchange notes in a special section included on each page. Teams of teachers also can keep a telephone directory and log by each team phone. They contain addresses and parents' work and home phone numbers, as well as a record of conversations with parents, so that all team members know the number and nature of the calls. Some teachers also send home a unit guide before each new unit begins so that parents know what is coming and can ask their children appropriate questions.

Tell parents about homework problems as soon as they arise. Parents are best able to work out a solution with the child and teacher if they know about the homework problem before report card are distributed.

School should have a real open-door policy. Parents should be welcome at any time. School should run like a family and the teachers should try to contact parents frequently with information about the good things their children are doing. That way they will return their call when a problem comes up. On the rare occasion when a homework problem becomes pesky, the teacher can sign a contract with the parent and child that spell out how the problem is to be fixed. Notes also go back and forth from school to home so that communication lines are kept open. The teachers can also use a monthly newsletter to parents to address any general problems such as incomplete homework that require their support.

Schools should have, as many do, homework policies published in both the faculty handbook and the parent/student handbook.

Some tips:

- There should be a clear policy statement, developed in consultation with the pupils, staff, parents and administrators and this should be reviewed on a regular basis.
- Staff and pupils should regard homework as an integral part of the curriculum—it is planned and prepared alongside all other programmes of learning.
- The foundations of effective homework practices should be established early on and develop progressively across the key stages—effective homework practices can also be used to support transitionary links to the secondary phase.

- Homework should be set and managed effectively.
- Schools approach to homework should be realistic.
- Homework tasks should be differentiated and appropriated to the needs of individuals.
- The support of parents and guardians should be seen as essential. They should assist in many ways, for instance helping their children at home, monitoring homework, providing encouragement and assisting with the marking of homework.
- Effective homework strategies should support a range of settings in which pupils learn, for example, through parental support and guidance, joint family learning tasks, to independent learning.
- Homework should be marked or graded according to the general school marking policy.
- The quality of completed homework should be monitored and reviewed at regular periods in consultation with pupils and parents.
- Homework competed well should be acknowledged and praised.
- Innovative homework practices should reflect developments within education and the range of learning styles, for instance, the use of ICT (Information Communication Technology) and Accelerated Learning.

Schools can get following things written on a display board for the visitors

Objectives of homework:

- To reinforce, maintain and extend classroom learning.
- To stimulate new learning.
- To increase the involvement of each student with learning task.
- To develop student responsibility, time management and self-confidence.
- To promote creativity.

- To establish communication between parent and child/ home and school on the importance of learning.
- To promote good study habits and techniques.

4.5 HOMEWORK AND ADMINISTRATORS

For homework to be considered an important means to success in all curricula, administrators need to be involved in the process. They are the educational leaders. Their leadership, support and encouragement will assist all parties in the pursuit of good homework practices.

All parents want their child to succeed so deciding to uphold the homework policy is not a difficult choice for parents. The administration's homework policy should provide guidelines for parental involvement, which will encourage parents to be part of the solution in helping students, succeed.

Administrative Responsibilities (Principal, Assistant, Supervisors) will:

- Review and monitor all teachers' homework guidelines, and make appropriate recommendations to teachers before the guidelines are communicated to the students.
- Place homework on the agenda at least once a year at their department meetings. This is for the purpose of exchanging ideas and giving each other feedback and information.
- Assist in the dissemination of the secondary school homework procedures and practices.
- Review homework procedures and practices periodically at faculty and supervisor meetings.
- Assist teachers, students and parents in following the school homework practices.
- Review and monitor all teachers' homework guidelines and make appropriate recommendations to teachers.
- Make school-designed assignment notebooks available for purchase at the start of each school year.
- Ensure that copies of all individual teachers' homework guidelines are on file in either the guidance department or the main office.

- Communicate the district (if any) and school homework policies to parents.
- Monitor the implementation of the policy.
- Co-ordinate the scheduling of homework among different subjects, if needed.

Administrators are responsible for:

- Ensuring that the school homework policy is published and circulated to all the concerned people for wide critical review and recommendations.
- Supporting teachers' efforts to ensure homework is completed.
- Planning for the periodic evaluation of the school homework policy by teachers, students and parents.
- To assist in the dissemination and implementation of the Homework Guidelines to all teachers, parents/guardians and students.
- To help to plain, clarify and interpret all parts of the guidelines and to assist in the mediation of disputes regarding homework practices.
- To consistently monitor the implementation of the homework guidelines to insure full compliance by all teachers.

Administrators' responsibilities at central and state levels:

- Department of Education of Govt. of India should develop a Homework policy which may be implemented at national level or which may work as model for the State Governments.
- In the process of development of homework policy at national level, various boards of education, NCERT, and Universities can be involved.
- State Government. should develop its own homework policy and communicate it to the education officials at the district level to be implemented in various schools.
- The policy should be suggestive not prescriptive in nature.

HOMEWORK RESEARCH AND RESEARCHERS

5

Many organizations have supported researchers in studying effective homework practices, and in return, they have produced findings to help students to participate and progress in the general education curriculum. The number and percentage of research documents containing references to homework indicate that scholars are more interested in homework now than ever before.

Some researchers have urged the schools to take a fresh look at homework and its potential for engaging students and improving student performance. The key, they say, is to take into account grade-specific and developmental factors when determining the amount and kind of homework. So, what is appropriate? What benefits can be expected? What makes for good homework policies? Research doesn't have all the answers, but a review of existing data yields some helpful observations and guidance.

Sample of Research Outcomes

- Teaching responsibility and time management are important and often used as reason for homework, but this learning can be done with simple tasks (Cooper, 1989, Butler, 1987 and Copple, 1992).
- The single most important thing that children can do to grow academically is to read (Copple, 1992 and Adelman, 1995). Thus, reading kind of homework has a great significance at least academically.

- Appropriate kinds and amounts of homework raise achievement levels for students above primary levels. Homework is most beneficial when it is:
  (a) Relevant to learning objectives.
  (b) Appropriate to students' ability and maturity levels.
  (c) Collected and reviewed during class.
  d) Supported by parents.
  (e) Assigned regularly.
  (f) Well explained and motivated.
  (g) Used as an occasion for giving feedback (Butler, 1987, Holmes & Cross, 1989, Hossler, Stage and Galaghes, Paschal, 1988, Weinstein and Walberg, 1984).
- How much homework a student should take, it is impossible to give a definite answer. How wisely a student uses practice time in class, the pace of work and the level of difficulty are variables unique to each individual. What is generally true, homework is a life skill and it enhances learning and responsibility.
- Public support for homework is favourable. Most teachers, parents and students say doing homework helps students perform better in school.
- Study finds telly addicts do poorer homework.
- Researchers have proved what parents and teachers have known all along — that doing homework in front of distractions (of any sort) is not a good idea.
- Homework for primary school children does not necessarily improve their performance, according to one of the researches. It is more valuable in secondary schools, but pupils who spend hours working every night do not always get better grades.
- Caroline Sharp (2001), of the National Foundation for Education Research, said studies on the benefit of homework for younger children were inconclusive and there was an urgent need for more in-depth research.

- Two British studies have shown that homework in secondary schools produced better exam results, but the influence was relatively small.
- Parents generally supported setting homework though it could be a cause of conflict.
- *The report, Homework*: A Review of Recent Research, said pupils with a positive attitude to homework were most likely to achieve (*Telegraph*, 28 June 2001).
- With the school year in full swing, children are being assigned homework, and parents are coping or facilitating its completion as best they can. Parents often have questions about why homework is assigned, how beneficial it is, and how they may best help their child complete homework. A recent study reported on five major themes of parents' thinking about homework: (1) concern about their child's unique characteristics as balanced with school demands, (2) questions about the appropriate level of independent work assigned to their child, (3) concerns about how they can best structure homework activities, (4) concerns about how involved they should be in helping their child complete homework, and (5) reflections on what it means to them when they are or are not successful at being able to help their children complete assignments (Hoover-Dempsey, Bassler and Burow, 1995).
- Corno (1996) reports five widespread misconceptions about homework. The best teachers give homework regularly. Actually, the best teachers vary homework assignments according to the task at hand, and many teachers view homework policies that state it must be assigned on a regular basis as undermining their curricular goals and personal teaching style.
- More homework is better than less. The amount of work assigned has not been proven to be a reliable indicator of increased academic performance.
- Parents want their children to have homework. Parents want their children to do well in school, but that desire

cannot be interpreted to mean that they want their children to have homework if it is not going to improve their academic achievement.

- Homework supports what students learn in school. Teachers give different reasons for why they assign homework, and many homework assignments do not serve to help students reorganize and extend their learning.
- Homework fosters discipline and personal responsibility. There is little evidence to support this widely held idea. Corno (1996) says that this finding is only "one small piece of the bigger pie" and that parents foster these characteristics in larger, broader ways than through "doing homework".
- Homework hotlines targeting secondary school students research offers recommendations for setting up successful hotline.
- Research shows homework does boost academic achievement; but overemphasizing grades/marks and performance may lead to cheating.
- The more homework students complete, especially from grades six to twelve, the better they do in school, according to research conducted by psychologists Harris Cooper, James J. Lindsay, and Scott Greathouse, of the University of Missouri — Columbia and psychologist Barbara Nye, of Tennessee State University (1998). The research also demonstrates that parental attitudes toward homework play an important role in their children's education.
- The study, which is the first to incorporate attitudinal measures into an analysis of the link between homework and achievement by examining the beliefs parents, teachers, and students hold regarding homework, represents an initial attempt to gather estimates of homework behaviour from three sources.
- The study relates teacher, student, and parent reports of the amount of homework teachers assigned and the

proportion of homework students completed to students' standardized test scores and class grades.

- The psychologists obtained complete data sets from over 700 "triads," which they defined as consisting of a teacher, at least one student in a teacher's class, and one parent of that student. Homework behaviour was analysed from students in second through twelfth grades.
- While the amount of homework completed by students was positively related to their achievement in school, the study demonstrates that the relationship between homework completed and achievement is strongest at upper grades and for teacher-assigned grades (as opposed to performance on standardized tests).
- At lower grades, teachers may determine the amount of homework they assign young students based on their own beliefs regarding its merit, yet the authors note that increased out-of-school assignments may lead to unfavourable attitudes toward homework among elementary school students. "Although the benefits of study at home for young children may not be immediately evident, we support assigning homework to younger elementary schoolchildren due to its potential long-term developmental impact, for it helps elementary school goers develop proper study skills, which, in turn, influence grades," says Dr. Cooper, lead author of the study. However, the authors advise that teachers should attempt to ensure that outside assignments are of a proper length for the developmental level of their students, since too much homework can lead to fatigue and academic disinterest.
- The authors note that parental attitudes with respect to study at home have direct, positive effects on their children's attitudes toward homework and, at upper grades, on their children's classroom achievement.
- Attitudes about homework may be transmitted from parent to child, and parental involvement in the homework process affects their child's education. The

authors assert, "Schoolteachers and educational policy-makers should interpret these results to mean that efforts to improve parental attitudes toward homework are likely to pay off" (Article: "Relationships Among Attitudes About Homework, Amount of Homework Assigned and Completed, and Student Achievement" by Harris Cooper, Ph.D., James J. Lindsay, Ph.D., and Scott Greathouse, Ph.D., University of Missouri—Columbia, and Barbara Nye, Ph.D., of Tennessee State University in *Journal of Educational Psychology*, Vol. 90, No. 1).

- Walberg (1986) has described results of 11 reviews of research on effects of instructional methods and teaching skills on student achievement. The instructional methods included individualized, special, and cooperative learning; ability grouping; direct and programmed instruction; advance organizers; higher-level cognitive questioning; use of praise; use of pre-tests; and television watching. For each strategy, Walberg calculated an effect (e.g., the average high school student doing homework outperformed 69 per cent of students not doing homework). In comparison with these instructional strategies, homework's effect on achievement can be described most accurately as above average. That is, homework's influence fell about in the middle of the strategies. If grade level is considered, the relation between homework and achievement of elementary school students is comparatively small, but on high school students homework's effect is large, relative to the effect of the other instructional techniques.
- Another means of interpreting the size of an effect is to compare it with the cost of implementing the treatment. Homework is definitely a low-cost treatment. The most significant costs involved in assigning homework would be (a) a slight loss in instructional class time because time must be set aside for dealing with homework, and (b) additional outside-class preparation and management time for teachers.

Future direction for research

- In addition to studying homework's overall effectiveness, researchers should examine how variation in assignments might influence their efficacy. One obvious question is whether homework is more effective for some subjects than for others.
- Researchers should conduct researches on the fact that whether academic performance is a function of increasing homework time at various levels such as elementary, secondary and senior secondary.
- Some researches should be conducted related to differences in homework assignments. For example, there may be considerable evidence that homework results in better achievement if material is distributed across several assignments rather than concentrated only on material covered in class that day. Homework that requires students to practice material already taught, as well as assignments meant to prepare students for upcoming lessons, both may prove beneficial.
- Studies on the parental involvement should be conducted. For example, is giving parents a formal role in homework affects its utility.
- Some studies should be conducted regarding individualizing homework assignments, which might have effect on achievement.
- Some researches should be conducted in which researchers compare a homework feedback strategy (e.g., grading, instruction, or evaluative comments) with a no-feedback approach.
- Some survey kind of research should be conducted on need and use of homework hotlines to find out effects on academic performance.
- Research into the costs and benefits of homework for pupils, parents and teachers at primary as well as secondary level.

- Studies using an experimental design to assess the effectiveness of different homework interventions, such as homework designed to encourage specific types of parental involvement, different types of homework tasks, use of homework planners and different approaches to making and getting feedback.
- Studies investigating the application of new technology in relation to homework.
- Research into the impact of homework on pupil attitudes.
- Research aimed at identifying effective homework practices for lower-achieving pupils and pupils with special educational needs.
- Studies focusing on the impact of the homework environment and form of task in relation to individual learning styles.
- Studies concerning the relationship between homework for young (primary age) children and the development of self-regulating learning.
- Future researches need to involve families that are typically underrepresented in homework studies.
- Additional studies should "broaden the nature of the criteria used to evaluate the effectiveness of homework. Also, certain intermediate outcomes, such as improved motivation and effective study habits should be used to assess the impact of homework, especially in younger students.
- The outcomes of homework can also be compared with those of other teaching methods. This will allow the consideration of homework in a wider educational context, thus permitting a more accurate judgement of its value.
- In addition to studying homework's overall effectiveness, researchers can also examine how variation in homework assignments may influence their efficacy.
- Since over 90 per cent of the study's respondents were White, the authors maintain that future researchers need

to involve families that are typically underrepresented in homework studies. Additional studies should "broaden the nature of the criteria used to evaluate the effectiveness of homework," and the psychologists contend that certain intermediate outcomes, such as improved motivation and effective study habits should be used to assess the impact of homework, especially in younger students.

- In the previous section I discussed the effect of homework across differing grade levels, types of outcomes, and content areas. The outcomes of homework can also be compared with those of other teaching methods. This allows the consideration of homework in a wider educational context, thus permitting a more accurate judgement of its value.
- Relationship among attitudes about homework amount of homework assigned and completed and student achievement.
- Homework's effects on achievement and attitudes.

Sample of Questionnaires, which may be helpful for the researchers going to conduct the research in the area of homework:

QUESTIONNAIRE FOR TEACHERS

Name:..

Qualification: ....

Designation: ....

Teaching Experience...

Classes taught:...

Teaching subject ....

Name of School: ....

School Address: ....

Phone: ....

Residential Address: ....

....

....

....

....

E-Mail Address (if any): ....

Notes:

- Please read all the questions carefully.
- Answer all the questions, as all questions are compulsory.
- Feel free to answer.
- Your response will not be revealed to anybody.
- Take sufficient time before answering a question.
- Please answer the following questions on your own.
- These questions are not to test your knowledge rather to find out the general trend prevalent.

Q-1 Do you think homework should be given?

(a) Yes (b) No (c) Occasionally

Q-2 Do you assign homework to your students daily?

(a) Yes (b) No (c) Occasionally

Q-3 Do you check your student's homework daily?

(a) Yes (b) No (c) Sometimes

Q-4 Do you give homework as a complement of your class teaching?

(a) Yes (b) No (c) Sometimes

Q-5 Do you give instruction to your students for related homework?

(a) Yes (b) No (c) Occasionally

Q-6 Do you encourage your students for doing their homework?

(a) Yes (b) No (c) Sometimes

Q-7 Do you tell the importance of doing homework to your students?

(a) Yes (b) No (c) Sometimes

Q-8 Do you question your students when they do not complete their homework?

(a) Yes (b) No (c) Sometimes

Q-9 Do you try to know the difficulties of your students in doing homework?

(a) Yes (b) No (c) Sometimes

Q-10 Do you try to remove the difficulties of your students in doing homework?

(a) Yes (b) No (c) Sometimes

Q-11 Do you give comments on notebook of students, when you check their homework?

(a) Yes (b) No (c) Occasionally

Q-12 Do you give feedback to the students' on the basis of notebook on present work?

(a) Yes (b) No (c) Occasionally

Q-13 Are you in favour of giving punishment to students when they do not complete their homework?

(a) Yes (b) No (c) Sometimes

Q-14 Do you suggest yours students to set a personal regular timetable for doing homework?

(a) Yes (b) No (c) Sometimes

Q-15 Do you consider any modification regarding homework assignment according to students' needs?

(a) Yes (b) No (c) Sometimes

Q-16 Do you teach and encourage students to use an assignment notebook and check it regularly?

(a) Yes (b) No (c) Sometimes

Q-17 What do you think about the nature of homework — a burden or a challenge for students?

(a) A burden (b) A challenge

Q-18 How do you perceive homework in your teaching — as a tool or as a weapon?

(a) A tool (b) A weapon

Q-19 Do you contact parents of your students regarding homework incompletion?

(a) Yes (b) No (c) Sometimes

Q-20 Do you assign same homework to all students?

(a) Yes (b) No (c) Sometimes

Q-21 Are you able to classify your students on the basis of their homework completion?

(a) Yes (b) No

Q-22 Do you co-ordinate assignments and tests with other teachers to avoid students overload?

(a) Yes (b) No (c) Sometimes

Q-23 What do you mean by homework?

....

....

....

....

....

Q-24 Why homework should be given?

....

....

....

....

....

Q-25 How homework is helpful in your students' learning?

....

....

....

....

....

Q-26 How do you encourage your students for doing their homework?

....

....

....

....

....

Q-27 How do you try to know the difficulties of students in doing homework?

....

....

....

....

....

Q-28 How do you remove the difficulties of students in doing homework?

....

....

....

....

....

Q-29 How do you tackle homework in your teaching — as a tool or as a weapon?

....

....

....

....

....

Q-30 What do you think about homework — a burden or a challenge for students?

....

....

....

....

....

Q-31 What do you think about the present trend of homework?

....

....

....

....

....

Q-32 Do you want some changes in present trend of homework? If yes, then what kind of changes you suggest?

....

....

....

....

....

Your Comments and Suggestions:

....

....

....

....

....

....

....

....

....

....

....

....

....

QUESTIONNAIRE FOR STUDENTS

Student's name: ....

Roll No.: ....

Class: .... Section: ....

Name of the School: ....

Residential address: ....

Contact No.: ....

E-mail: ....

Notes:

- Please read all the questions carefully.
- Answer all the questions, as all questions are compulsory.
- Feel free to answer.
- Your response will not be revealed to anybody.
- Take sufficient time before answering a question.
- Please answer the following questions honestly on your own.
- These questions are not to test your knowledge rather to find out the general trend prevalent.

Q-1 Do you think homework should be given daily or not?

(a) Yes (b) No (c) Occasionally

Q-2 Do you have homework every school day?

(a) Yes (b) No (c) Occasionally

Q-3 Do you usually have homework on weekends?

(a) Yes (b) No (c) Occasionally

Q-4 Only typical school day, I usually have homework

(a) In one or two subjects

(b) In three or four subjects

(c) In more than four subjects

(Please list the subject you have the most homework in.)

Q-5 Please describe the type of homework you typically have (circle all that apply)

(a) Completing class work

(b) Reading from the text.

(c) Answering questions, taking notes, working practice problems.

Q-6 Do you do homework daily?

(a) Yes (b) No (c) Occasionally

Q-7 How long do you typically spend each day/night doing homework?

(a) One to two hours

(b) Two to three hours

(c) Three to four hours

(d) Over four hours

Q-8 What time do you usually begin homework?

....

Q-9 What time do you usually complete your homework/studying?

....

Q-10 Do you participate in co-curricular activities after school? Yes/no

If yes, please mention the activities?

....

Q-11 Are you being tutored? Yes/no.

If yes, please answer the following regarding tutoring.

I am being tutored through

(a) An independent tutor.

(b) Student support services by school

(c) How many days in a week? ....

Q-12 If you are not tutored who assist you in completing homework.

(a) Parents (b) Elder brother/sister

(c) Friends (d) Neighbours

Q-13 Is it easy to contact your teacher outside of school to seek help to do your homework?

(a) Yes (b) No (c) Occasionally

Q-14 Are you punished for not doing homework?

(a) Yes (b) No (c) Occasionally

Q-15 What do you think about homework?

(a) Homework is a burden

(b) Homework is an enjoyment

(c) Sometimes a burden/sometimes an enjoyment

Q-16 Does homework help you in your study?

(a) Yes (b) No (c) Occasionally

Q-17 Do you feel some difficulties in doing homework?

(a) Yes (b) No (c) Occasionally

Q-18 What do you feel when you completed your homework successfully in given time?

(a) Confident (b) Not-confident

(c) Nothing special

Q-19 Do you take the help of other material like guide, help book in doing your homework?

(a) Yes (b) No (c) Occasionally

Q-20 What is the attitude of your parents towards your homework?

(a) Positive (b) Negative (c) Indifferent

Q-21 Do you set a regular timetable for doing homework?

(a) Yes (b) No

Q-22 Do you think some changes are required in the trend of assigning homework?

(a) Yes (b) No

Q-23 Why do you think that homework should be given daily?

....

....

....

....

....

Q-24 Are you satisfied with the homework that is given to you in your school?

....

....

....

....

....

Q-25 How your parents help you in completion of homework?

....

....

....

....

....

Q-26 What difficulties do you face during homework completion?

....

....

....

....

....

Q-27 Do you take help of other resources for completion of your homework? What are these?

....

....

....

....

....

Q-28 Does your teacher give extra suggestions for the related homework?

....

....

....

....

....

Q-29 What do you feel while you are doing your homework?

....

....

....

....

....

Q-30 What kind of suggestion/help you expect from your teacher when they assign you homework?

....

....

....

....

....

Q-31 How helpful is your homework in your study?

....

....

....

....

....

Q-32 What type of changes you want in present trend of homework?

....

....

....

....

Your Comments and Suggestions:

....

....

....

....

....

....

....

....

....

....

....

....

....

....

QUESTIONNAIRE FOR PARENTS

Name of the father/guardian: ....

Qualification: .... Occupation: ....

Name of the mother: ....

Qualification: .... Occupation: ....

Residential Address: ....

....

....

Phone and E-mail: ....

Notes:

- Please read all the questions carefully.
- Answer all the questions, as all questions are compulsory.
- Feel free to answer.
- Your response will not be revealed to anybody.
- Take sufficient time before answering a question.

- Please answer the following questions honestly on your own.
- These questions are not to test your knowledge rather to find out the general trend, prevalent.

Q-1 Do you think homework should be given?
(a) Yes (b) No (c) Occasionally

Q-2 Do you check whether homework is given to your child regularly or not?
(a) Yes (b) No (c) Occasionally

Q-3 Do you observe that your child completes his/her homework or not?
(a) Yes (b) No (c) Occasionally

Q-4 Do you help your child when he/she faces difficulty in doing his/her homework?
(a) Yes (b) No (c) Occasionally

Q-5 Do you provide guidance to your child in completing his/her homework when your child asks for help?
(a) Guidance (b) answer (c) as per need

Q-6 Have you developed strategy for dealing with homework for your child?
(a) Yes (b) No (c) Occasionally

Q-7 Do you praise your child, when he/she successfully completes his/her homework?
(a) Yes (b) No (c) Occasionally

Q-8 Do you give some additional work to your child related to his/her class study?
(a) Yes (b) No (c) Occasionally

Q-9 Do you think that your help or observance is more important for your child than a tutor?
(a) Yes (b) No (c) Occasionally

Q-10 Do you arrange a proper place for doing homework for your child?
(a) Yes (b) No

Q-11 Do you show interest in your child homework assignment?
(a) Yes (b) No (c) Occasionally

Q-12 Do you arrange your child to have a regular timetable for doing homework?
(a) Yes (b) No (c) Occasionally

Q-13 What is your attitude towards your child's homework?
(a) Positive (b) Negative (c) Indifferent

Q-14 Do you see that assignments are started and completed by your child?
(a) Yes (b) No (c) Occasionally

Q-15 Do you understand and respect your child style of learning? Is he better alone or with someone's?
(a) Yes (b) No (c) Occasionally

Q-16 Do you like to arrange a group of learning children so that they should do their homework together?
(a) Yes (b) No

Q-17 Do you read the teacher's comments on assignments that are returned?
(a) Yes (b) No (c) Occasionally

Q-18 Do you put yourself as a role model taking the opportunity to read a book or newspaper when your child studies?
(a) Yes (b) No (c) Occasionally

Q-19 Do you try to relate the homework to your child's everyday life?
(a) Yes (b) No (c) Occasionally

Q-20 Are you interested to meet your child's teacher about his/her homework problems?
(a) Yes (b) No (c) Occasionally

Q-21 How many times you visit your child's school on calling by his/her class teacher?
(a) Yes (b) No (c) Occasionally

Q-22 Do you inform the class teacher about your child's weaknesses in doing his/her homework?

(a) Yes (b) No (c) Occasionally

Q-23 Why homework should be given?

....

....

....

....

....

Q-24 What is the need and importance of homework in your child's education?

....

....

....

....

....

Q-25 What questions you ask to your child when he says that, "today I don't have any homework?"

....

....

....

....

....

Q-26 How do you observe your child when he is doing his homework?

....

....

....

....

....

Q-27 How do you teach your child to be organized in his study time or doing homework?

....

....

....

....

....

Q-28 While helping your child to complete his homework, how do you assist him? (Taking help from notes, guides etc.)

....

....

....

....

....

Q-29 When your child asks for help in completing homework, you provide guidance or answers to him/her?

....

....

....

....

....

Q-30 What do you think about homework — a burden or a challenge for your child?

....

....

....

....

....

Q-31 What do you think about present pattern of homework?

....

....

....

....

....

Q-32 Do you think some changes should be brought in policies and practices of homework? What type of changes do you suggest?

....

....

....

....

....

Your Comments and Suggestions:

....

....

....

....

....

....

....

....

....

....

....

....

HOMEWORK AND TEACHER EDUCATION PROGRAMME

6

Homework plays a significant role in education in every nation of the world. But, it is surprising how little or no significant attention is paid to the topic of homework in teacher education programme. Most teachers in India report that in education courses they discussed homework in relation to specific subject, but received little training in how to devise good homework assignments, how to decide how much homework to assign and how to involve parents in homework process. The fact is that in the entire curriculum of teacher education, concept of homework finds no respectable place at all. Consequently when the teacher actually enters in the practical arena of education, he/she finds totally helpless while deciding what type of homework assignment would be appropriate in a given situation as he/she has hardly any idea what are the types of homework and what are its characteristics. He/she has no clue how to make homework assignment as creative one?, how to use homework assignments to develop and retain the involvement of parents in students' learning?, how to make sure that students understand the purpose of homework?, how to make assignment focused and clear?, how to match assignments to his or her (teacher) style of teaching?, how to make homework varied which may suit to special needs of the students?, how to create assignments that challenge students to think and to integrate?, etc. At the same time when parents approach to the teachers with their questions and concerns, teachers find themselves in baffling situation.

Rich (1997) agrees that teachers have a responsibility when assigning homework to "let kids know what you are teaching through the homework and why". But, she finds that "this isn't typically taught" in pre-service teacher education programme — a professional development programme devoted to teacher preparation. What also is not taught, says Russo (1997) is the power homework has to engage parents in the school life. "Teachers need to consider how parents can contribute to a child's development, she contends. The curriculum of Teacher Education Programme must have "homework education" as one of its contents through which pupil teachers may be exposed to various theoretical and practical facets of homework assignments. Pupil teachers should be made attitudinally constructive and purposive that homework is home-links in the sense that it bridges the school and home. Through home-links, parents have an opportunity to reinforce learning, to become involved in their child's education.

Is it really true that homework does not figure at all in the teacher education curriculum? No. Not as such. While imparting knowledge regarding how to develop a lesson plan in any subject, it does figure. Let us have a look at lesson plan format largely in use in different Teacher Education Colleges/ Institutes/University Department of Education etc.

Lesson Plan Format

Lesson Plan No. .....

Subject:	School:
Topic:	Class:
Sub-topic:	No. of students:
	Age group:
	Period:
	Duration:

1. General Aims:
2. General Objectives:

3. Specific Objectives:

4. Teaching Aids:

5. Introduction:

6. Previous knowledge testing:

7. Announcement of the lesson:

8. Presentation:

Specific Objectives	Pupil-Teacher's Activity	Students' Activity

9. Recapitulation:

10. Homework Assignments:

Every teacher educator devotes a good amount of time and energy to explain every step and components of lesson planning from general aims, objective, specific objective (particularly instructional objectives), — to recapitulation. But, under the heading of homework, pupil-teachers are left own their own without any proper directions. They are simply told to write homework on the basis of the lesson to be taught. That is all. No detail discussions take place around the questions like —

what is homework?, what are its types?, what is its need and importance?, how to develop effective guidelines for the students as well as parents?, how to assist the school administrators to develop homework policy?, etc.

During even micro-teaching programme, every skill development is taken well care of. Skills like — introduction, questioning, explaining, stimulation variation, etc. are discussed and practiced with all sincerity. But, no adequate attention is paid towards homework as a skill.

Homework Skill

It is a skill, which will enable the pupil-teacher to have a deeper insight regarding homework assignments. The pupil-teacher will become efficient in designing, assigning, and evaluating homework. Also, he/she will be in position to use homework assignments to develop and retain the involvement of parents in students' learning, to make sure students understand the purpose of homework, to make assignment focused and clear, to match assignments to his/her (teacher) style of teaching, to make homework varied which may suit to special needs of the students, to create assignments that challenge students to think and to integrate etc.

Characteristic of Homework-skill

Some characteristics are as under:

- It is not a method of classroom instruction rather a technique/skill.
- It is an individualized training device.
- This training device is an aid to teaching and learning.

Objectives of Homework-skill

- To provide a practice to the pupil-teachers how to draft homework assignment before assigning it to students.
- To identify the drawbacks of the pupil-teachers and to give immediate feedback for modifying their developing/drafting/assigning skills.
- To improve their understanding towards homework which appears so simple but complex in nature.

Objectives of introducing Homework-skill in Teacher Education

- To initiate the pupil-teacher to develop a deeper understanding about the nature and types of homework, why homework should be assigned.
- To enable the pupil-teachers to understand the need and importance of homework as an intellectual discipline and as a skill also.
- To enable the pupil-teachers how to design and assign homework with a definite purpose based on the types of homework assignment (Practice, Preparation, Extension, Application, Creative and Cooperative).
- To enable the pupil-teachers how to design homework assignments so that it may reinforce classroom instruction, increase understanding and retention, transfer extended classroom instruction, prepare for class discussion and provide curriculum enriched opportunities.
- To enable the pupil-teachers to help the administrators in development of homework policy.
- To enable the pupil-teachers to help and guide the students to complete the homework assignments without any great difficulty.
- To enable the pupil-teachers to help the parents when they approach them with the queries like "How can I help my child with his or her homework?", "How to adapt homework assignments to maximize child's strength?", "How much help with homework is appropriate?", "How to help the child struggling to manage difficult or long-term assignments?", "How to help child make a dull or boring homework task more enjoyable?", "What to do when the child doesn't understand the homework?", What to do when the child takes too long to complete homework?, What to do when our child rushes through homework and makes careless errors?, etc.
- To enable the pupil-teachers to help promote continuity and consistency with homework practices.

- To enable the pupil-teachers to help promote and foster positive experiences about homework.
- To enable the pupil-teachers to help increase the land of communication between home and school, especially as it relates to homework assignments.
- To enable the pupil-teachers to encourage children to develop the skills, confidence and motivation to study effectively on their own.
- To enable the pupil-teachers to develop and retain the involvement of parents in their own children's learning.
- To enable the pupil-teachers to keep parents informed about the work the children are doing at schools.
- To enable the pupil-teachers to make the students aware of their school's homework policy.
- To enable the pupil-teachers to make the children able to use extra resources for learning at home—e.g., computer, internet, library, adult knowledge etc.
- To enable the pupil-teachers to encourage children as they get older to develop the confidence and self-discipline needed to study on their own.
- To enable the pupil-teachers to help the students consolidate and reinforce the skills developed in lessons, to extend scope of learning and thus, to raise standards.
- To enable the pupil-teachers to guide students to develop student's initiative confidence and motivate research and study skills.
- To enable the pupil-teachers to help students become independent, autonomous, and motivated learner prepared for lifelong learning.

Assumptions of Homework-skill

- It will be possible to see whether pupil-teachers have developed the competency or not as far as various facets of homework assignments are concerned.
- It will be possible to find out the drawbacks (if any) in assigning and designing the homework and then they

can be improved upon. For example, when the pupil-teachers are writing the homework assignment in the lesson plan whether they are aware of various components of homework or not.

- It will be possible to provide necessary understanding for homework-skill very well by rigorous exercises.
- Feedback to the pupil-teachers can be possible immediately so that they may develop necessary skills required for the development, implementation and evaluation of homework assignments.

Phases of Homework-skill

- *Knowledge acquisition phase*: This phase provides the pupil-teachers to get knowledge of homework as a discipline and as a skill. They are advised to scan the literature related with homework keeping in mind that those related information they are going to utilize in the development of homework as a skill. They are made to do the practice of writing/assigning the homework under the guidance of an expert who understands the ins and outs of homework assignments. The pupil-teachers get the theoretical as well as practical aspects of knowledge of homework-skill.
- *Skill acquisition phase*: The pupil-teachers acquire the homework-skill through a lot of practice. On the basis of a given content, the pupil-teachers are required to develop a homework assignment and get it checked (The checking is done with the help of rating scales) by the subject-teacher and through feedback they evaluate their performance. Then they rewrite/reassign the homework assignment with modification and improvement. This process is continued till they achieve the mastery over the homework-skill.
- *Transfer phase*: When the pupil-teachers go to schools for practice teaching in a real situation, they use the skill effectively. They assign the homework on the basis of different aspects of homework. From the assignment, it

is reflected that what kind of assignment has been assigned, what is purpose behind it, how this assignment is going to help the students either to practice already learnt knowledge in the class, prepare for the next class, extend the learnt knowledge, apply the learnt knowledge in a knew situation or create some thing new on the basis of learnt knowledge.

Procedure adopted in developing Homework-skill

- *Intensive discussion about homework*: A discussion is held about homework. Various facts and figures are discussed. Theory and practices of homework is discussed in great length so that the pupil teachers can acquaint themselves with the various concepts involved in homework such as what is homework and what are its need and importance, what are various types of homework, advantages and disadvantages of homework, homework policy and resources, different stakeholders of homework, etc.
- *Explaining the designing, assigning and evaluating homework*: Ways of designing/developing and assigning the homework are explained by the expert teacher. The pupil-teachers are provided with an explanation how to evaluate the completed assignments with desirable feedbacks.
- *Demonstrating the skill by the expert teacher*: One demonstration is given by the expert to the pupil-teachers.
- *Discussion and clarification*: After the demonstration, discussion takes place wherein the pupil-teachers discuss the things and seek all type of clarifications.
- *Practice of designing/developing the homework*: Selecting some contents, they start practicing of designing/ developing the homework.
- *Getting it checked*: The designed/developed homework is got checked by the teacher with the help of observation cum rating scales.

- *Feedback*: Immediately after the checking, the expert teacher provides the feedback for the improvement of designing/developing homework assignments.
- *Re-practice of designing/developing the homework*: Re-practice of designing/developing takes place.
- *Rechecking*: Rechecking by the expert takes place.
- *Re-feedback*: Re-feedback is provided by the expert to the pupil-teachers.
- This process may be continued till it is found that the pupil-teachers have achieved some level of mastery.

Components of Homework-skill

- Types of homework
- Purpose/objectives of homework
- Duration/length
- Adequacy of contents
- Degree of variation
- Degree of individualization
- Degree of choice

Observation cum rating scale:

COMPONENTS	RATING SCALE	REMARKS
Types of homework	0 1 2 3 4 5 6	
Purpose/objectives of homework	0 1 2 3 4 5 6	
Duration/length	0 1 2 3 4 5 6	
Adequacy of contents	0 1 2 3 4 5 6	
Degree of variation	0 1 2 3 4 5 6	
Degree of individualization	0 1 2 3 4 5 6	
Degree of choice	0 1 2 3 4 5 6	

Homework-skill Cycle

The following cycle will be repeated until the pupil-teacher gets mastery over homework-skill.

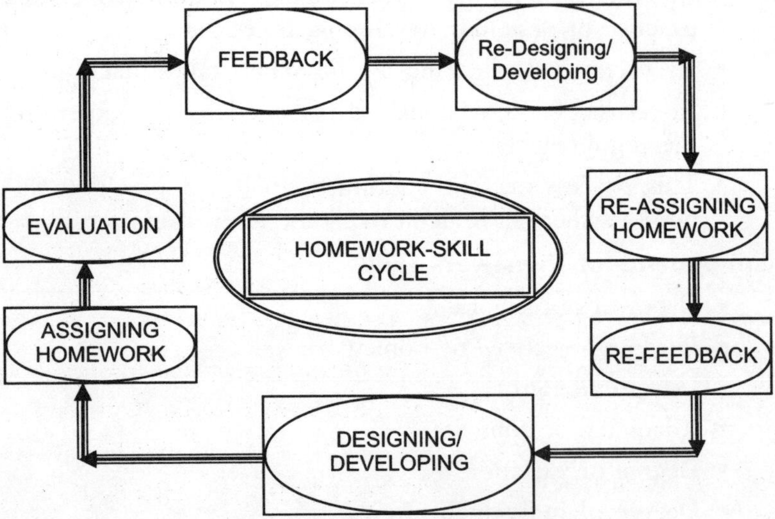

(Diagrammatic Representation)

What Teacher Education Programme should do?

- "Homework Education" as an intellectual discipline can be introduced.
- "Homework Education" can be introduced as a compulsory or optional paper.
- Every syllabus of teaching subject (Teaching of Mathematics, Physical Science, Life-Science, Social Science, Languages etc.) should have Homework as one of the major contents.
- Homework as a skill should be given a serious thought. Can we introduce, develop and practice something like that?
- Some modules should be developed to introduce homework as a discipline in Teacher education programme.

GENERAL STRATEGIES

7

- The ultimate impact of homework practices on students may depend largely on how favourably teachers, parents and the students themselves perceive them. There is the need to check out practices with all stakeholders.
- In today's modern world, an old-fashioned approach to homework won't work. Teachers have to 'sell' homework and make it relevant to students' lives. Schools will have to seek active parental support for homework and show parents how to reinforce, at home, what students learn in the classroom.
- Homework should have different purposes at different grades. For younger students, it should foster positive attitudes, habits and character traits. For older student, it should facilitate knowledge acquisition in specific topics.
- Homework should be required at all grade levels, but a mixture of mandatory and voluntary homework is most beneficial.
- Homework should be: (i) respectful of the child's ability and developmental level, (ii) related to the work of the classroom (clearly worded) and where possible, to the interest of the individual student and (iii) reasonable in amount and degree of difficulty.
- This does not mean that teachers need to create different homework assignments for every student every day, of course. There are obviously some assignments that everyone has to do and can easily accomplish, like writing or practicing a particular task.

- Specific differentiation is needed, for those students whose ability or work ethic is in need of support. There may be a student, for example, who struggles with mathematical problems. For this student, completing the standard homework assignment of fifteen mathematical problems could mean two hours of arduous task as opposed to the half an hour it takes for most. Anticipating this, the teacher might adjust the length of the assignment accordingly.
- There is every need to involve parents. Now the question arises how to do it? The most important strategy for involving parents is to inform them about homework expectations and practices. Clearly, the more informed parents are about homework expectations, the better able they will be to help their children meet these expectations.
- The school in general and an individual teacher in particular can send a letter to parents at the beginning of the school year explaining homework policy and expectations and enlisting parent support.
- Having students complete their first homework assignments at school and bringing them home to share with their family will also help parents gain a clear understanding of homework expectations.
- Teachers and parents of students must communicate clearly and effectively with one another and with students about homework policies, required practices, mutual expectations, student performance on homework, homework completion difficulties and other homework related concerns. Unfortunately, too often, communication is either unclear or not present.
- The research shows that there are problems in the following areas: initiation of communication, timeliness of communication, frequency of consistency of communication, follow-through and clarity and usefulness of the information. There is need to pay proper attention to all these areas.

- Research strengthens the case for homework. Studies generally have found homework assignments to be most helpful if they are carefully planned by the teachers and have direct meaning to students.
- Teachers, students and parents have the responsibility to work as a team in order to realize the maximize benefit of homework.
- A systematic approach to homework that clearly defines the role of administration, teachers, parents and students can increase the frequency of desired results. It is essential that all individuals assume specific responsibilities.
- If we are to increase students' success with homework, we must be willing to be flexible and to individualize assignments.
- Differentiated homework, like differentiated instruction, will be more work for the teacher in the short run, but the long-term pay off of student success and investment will be worth it.
- In the world-order of today, it is expected that all schools, in consultation with their communities, should review their existing school homework policy to ensure it is relevant to the needs of their students.
- On the basis of above exercises, a copy of the revised document should be distributed to staff, students, parents and other relevant people particularly at the time of student enrolment.
- Parents and other concerned people have an important role in assisting the school in this view of their school's homework policy. It has the potential to affirm the partnership in learning between parents and teachers and to ensure that the importance of family and leisure activities is recognised in the amounts and type of homework that is set.
- Full consideration should be given to the value and purpose of homework and the principles and practices outlined in this document that ensure homework is

educationally beneficial and meets the realistic expectations of students, teachers, parents and other people concerned.

Homework is most beneficial when

- It reinforces and extends class work and consolidates basic skills and knowledge.
- It is challenging and purposeful, but not so demanding that it has adverse effects on the student's motivation.
- Parents or guardians are involved in the formulation and implementation of the school's homework policy.
- Students take responsibility for their homework, supported by their parents or guardians.
- It is well coordinated and teacher expectations are well communicated.
- It is set on a regular basis and establishes a routine of human study.
- Teachers set suitable amounts of homework, which are varied, and at an appropriate level considering the age, stage of schooling and capabilities of students.
- It takes into account students' home responsibilities and co-curricular activities such as clubs, sport and part-time employment.
- It is marked promptly and accurately.
- Feedback and follow-up are provided regularly to students.
- It develops and extends the core learning skills of inquiry and independent study.
- Whenever possible homework should recognise the place of technology in today's world and the benefits of using technology such as home computers, E-mail and the Internet for organizing and accessing information. Schools however should have regard for equity issues when setting homework that relies upon the use of technology. Students who do not have access to such technology at home should not be disadvantaged.

- Educationists are demanding that at Pre-primary and primary stages, teachers should not set formal homework. However, all activities at home or in play can assist children to develop a wide range of knowledge and skills including literacy, numeric and problem-solving. Language and number concepts can be including: (a) shopping; (b) preparation of food; (c) listening to stories, learning songs and nursery rhymes; (d) conversations about what is happening at school; (e) interactive video and computer programmes; (f) reading; (g) library borrowing; (h) family outings; (i) collecting items etc.
- In the later stages of pre-primary consideration should be given to the setting of formal homework as for example in completing simple computations, copying letters or words or completing an activity sheet.
- Although as students progress they increasingly work independently on their homework, it is important that teachers continue to provide guidance and assistance particularly in the development of study skills.
- It is also important that students have the opportunity to experience different types of homework and that the amounts of time students are expected to work on homework is realistic.
- Although most homework is likely to be set in the areas of English, Mathematics, Science, Social-science etc., it could be set across all areas of the curriculum.
- In secondary schools, homework should develop in students, habits of reviewing work undertaken in class. It is expected that homework will be set on a regular basis in each subject. Coordination across faculties is essential to accommodate competing demands in regard to homework, assessment tasks, assignments and examination preparation. This is particularly important in the senior years of senior secondary schools.

- There are times when students should be provided with the opportunity to negotiate the amount, type and timeframes of homework.
- The quality of homework will be enhanced by students getting expert advice about homework and study skills through seminars and study days. This is important right across secondary school, not only in senior years.
- Many schools may find homework diaries useful to develop students' organizational skills and time management and to improve home-school communication.
- We cannot keep assigning homework. We need to look at the kids with a different perspective and come up with an approach to homework that respects their lives.
- Flexible assignments are important because we have some students who have access to every resource; at the same time we have some students who have nothing.
- A little creativity goes a long way in designing homework that is relevant to students' lives.
- Every school should develop something like Homelinks programme. The Homelinks programme may ask parents to guide students through the thirty minutes of homework assigned each night except Sunday or specific holidays. Each night's homework may focus on a different content area.
- The Homelinks programme may also feature presenting workshops that teach parents how to best help their children complete homework assignments.
- In the 'planner' in which students note their homework, there should be some space for parents to write their comments about what is happening in the classroom and how they think their children are responding.
- The planners will help the students to learn to ask: what did I accomplish today and what will I do tomorrow? The planners can teach them how to plan. And teaching

students how to plan is important because they will need that skill as adults.

- Teachers should create such homework assignments that are "interactive" and to include activities children can do with their parents or older siblings.
- Cooperative type of homework assignments should be assigned more and more. This kind of assignments may be a real fun for the students. Also, such homework assignments — those that require students to use natural materials — are enjoyed by them the most.
- There is need to have a national guidelines on homework.
- Coordinated policies should exist at the district, school and classroom levels. District Education Officer should offer a clear and broad rationale for assigning homework, including why it is sometimes mandatory, as well as general guidelines for the amount of how that should be assigned.
- Every school should have clear-cut homework policy.
- Schools need to provide more specific time requirements, coordinate assignments between classes and describe the role of teachers and principals.
- Students should have some opportunity to contribute to the development of the homework policies.
- Homework policies and practices should be moderately flexible and designed to promote student learning.
- Consequences for incomplete homework should be firm but respectful.
- Homework timetables should be prepared in consultation with subject co-ordinators. This timetable should be given to the pupils on the first day of the session and also can be made available to parents. Staffs are expected to set homework strictly in accordance with the published timetables.
- During lessons teaching staffs are requested to ensure that all homework details are written down at the time that the homework is set. Personal organizers should

also be used for forward planning and recording special instructions pertinent to the next lessons.

- Every school should have Homework Guidance Centre where teachers will inform the Centre head as what has been given to the students as homework assignments in the class. Also, this centre will guide and help the students as well as parents regarding homework difficulties. The centre must keep all the necessary information regarding homework, such as homework policy, homework timetables, information regarding various homework resources etc.
- In every school, a Homework Club should be formed.
- Schools should offer after school programmes in which homework is a major activity.
- After school programme staff can do many things to enhance accurate homework completion for students.
  - Communicate with the day school staff. Administrators should arrange for day staff to meet after school staff.
  - Facilitate ongoing communication between the day staff, after school staff and parents by using homework notebooks.
  - Use older students as helper.
  - Build instruction in study skills and learning strategies into the homework programme.
- We need to make sure that all students feel a valued part of their learning community and this includes how they participate in homework.
- If homework is assigned, it must be completed; it should not be optional, but rather integral to the instructional programme. A school's homework policy should convey the importance the school attaches to homework and emphasize student commitment and responsibility for completing it.

- Students must be able to complete assignments independently.
- Homework should be appropriate to completion at home.
- Teachers should distinguish between completion and effort.
- Teachers should coordinate major assignments.
- Teachers should help parents help their children.
- Homework should be geared towards the work of the classroom and where possible, to the interest of the child. It should be reflective of the child's ability and be developmentally appropriate.
- Teachers should try to make homework stimulating rather than a repetition of the day's in-class work.
- Giving choices for how homework is to be completed, sending home a list to parents of expectations and goals and using a reward and tracking system for homework completion are helpful ways to ensure participation.
- It is important that teachers monitor homework progress and communicate with the family regularly.
- Teachers should prepare children for homework because it is a teachable skill.
- Interviews with parents have cited lack of information about the curriculum and lack of information about the curriculum reforms. Responsible parents may be concerned that this lack of information would hamper their efforts to help their children. Thus, parents must be informed well in advance.
- Parents prefer for homework that is tailored to the individual child and that respect child and family needs. They are very clear in perception that there is no point in assigning someone an assignment that they cannot possibly do. Every parent prefers homework that involved concrete, authentic projects that are motivating for children.

Some guidelines

- Elementary school students should be assigned homework, though it should not be expected to improve their achievement. Rather, homework should help young children good study habits, promote positive attitude toward school and communicate to students that learning takes place outside as well as inside school. Thus, assignments to elementary students should be brief, should involve materials commonly found in the home and should not be too demanding.
- The academic function of homework should emerge in secondary school. However, at the same time, its use as a motivational tool should not be ignored. Thus, both required and voluntary assignments should be used. The latter should involve tasks that are intrinsically interesting to students of the age.
- Teachers should never use homework as punishment. Using it in this way communicates to students that schoolwork is boring and aversive.
- Secondary school teachers can view the home as an extension of the classroom. Homework that involves practice and review of lesson previously taught and a simple introduction to material prior to its coverage in class is desirable. Assignments that require students to integrate skills or differing parts of the curriculum should also be common.
- Regardless of students' ages, the formal role of parents in homework should be minimal. Parents vary in interest, knowledge, teaching skills and time available. Clearly, parents of young children should be more involved. In particular, they need opportunities to express how much they value school achievement. Besides helping their children to practice of reading, spelling and math skills, parents can express their interest by having contracts with their children about study times, offering rewards for completed assignments, or merely by signing homework before it is returned to school.

- Teachers should individualize few assignments within classes. Developing individualized homework demands considerable teacher time and has few benefits. Teachers who teach the same course to several classes that are progressing at different rates might consider giving the same assignments to the top students in the lowest class and the lowest-performing students in the highest class.
- Most homework assignments should not be graded. Teachers should not view homework as an opportunity to test. Almost all students should complete assignments successfully; thus, teachers should not differentiate much among performance levels. Having students do homework out of fear of negative consequences turns a situation ideal for building intrinsic motivation into one that implies that the teacher believes students need rewards or punishment in order to complete assignments. Teachers should collect homework, check it for completeness and give intermittent instructional feedback. This procedure shows that the teacher takes homework seriously and that it is purposeful. The major purpose should be to identify individual student's learning problems.
- In schools where different subjects are taught by different teachers, teachers should know:
  - What days of the week are available to them for assignments?
  - How much daily homework time should be spent on their subject?
- Teachers should state clearly:
  - How the assignment is related to the topic under study.
  - The purpose of the assignment.
  - How the assignment might best be carried out.
  - What the student must do to demonstrate the assignment has been completed.

Administrators should:

- Communicate the district (if any) and school homework policies to parents.
- Monitor the implementation of the policy.
- Co-ordinate the scheduling of homework among different subjects, if needed.

For students to be able to achieve the intended goals of homework assignments, communication between students, parents and teachers is essential. The following procedures are suggested:

- At the beginning of the school year the homework guidelines (if any, if there is no one, there is needed to develop one) should be distributed to all parents. Parents and teachers should be asked to review the guidelines and expectations with students.
- Each school should have an open forum that may provide an additional opportunity for presentation, review and clarification of the homework guidelines between teachers and parents.
- At the beginning of the school year, individual teachers should inform parents in writing of all homework expectations and procedures regarding the assessment in their classrooms.
- Parents are urged to contact their child's teacher when there are concerns about homework.
- Teachers are encouraged to use the meetings to solicit input from the parents/guardians of all students concerning the amount of time being spent on homework and any problem being encountered on a regular basis.
- In grades in which they are used, student assignment notebooks are useful tools for parents and teachers to communicate in writing as needed. Parents' signatures on homework, tests or other student work may be required to facilitate communication between home and school. Parent co-operation is necessary with this requirement.

- Students should be encouraged to use different homework resources for occasional questions or problem regarding homework.
- Generally extending a school vacation should be discouraged as it interferes with the teaching-learning process. This way it can be ensured that students will not miss work planned as part of their comprehensive educational experience as classroom interaction cannot be recaptured. Schoolwork missed due to family vacations or extended vacation (due to some family function and social obligations like attending marriages etc.) should be handled in the following manner.
  - Parents/guardians should notify the office and classroom teacher(s) of the dates that a child would be absent from school due to a family vacation or extended vacation.
  - During the absence from school, teachers will save homework and when appropriate, daily classroom work.
  - Upon returning from a family vacation or extended vacation the teacher will provide each child with a folder of make-up work to be completed.
  - Completed classroom work and homework is due no later than one week after the child's return to school.

SOME CONTENTIONS

8

Each piece of work is meaningful and valuable as it adds a new dimension to the corpus of knowledge and showers some new light in the field of education. In this way, the present work is also quite valuable as it is a small contribution to the studies done in the field of homework education and especially in relation to teaching and learning from the perspective of all the stakeholders of education. The following are major contentions.

Homework is valuable:

1. From the perspective of classroom teaching and learning, homework enables children to cover topics taught more thoroughly and with greater speed and accuracy and so that the activity of self-study becomes a natural complement of teaching.
2. Homework checking by the teachers can provide an opportunity to both the teachers and the students to identify, which area is stronger or which area is weaker among the major components of cognitive domain such as knowledge, understanding, application and skill.
3. Homework is important for the students as it can develop good habits and attitudes. It can also help students to work independently, encourage self-discipline and personal responsibility.
4. Homework can bring parents and teachers closer together; parents who supervise homework and assist their children with assignments learn more about their children's education and about the school.

5. Well-planned formulated, appropriate and purposeful homework is potential enough to reinforce, maintain and extend classroom learning.

Purposes of homework

1. *Practice/Review*: To reinforce and/or master basic skill already presented in class.
2. *Preparation*: To introduce material to be presented in future lessons.
3. *Extension*: To provide students with opportunities to transfer specific skills or concepts to new situation.
4. *Application*: To enable students to connect skills and concepts to novel circumstances.
5. *Creativity*: To enable students to be creative by performing certain tasks.

What is homework?

1. Homework is defined as a cost-effective instructional technique. It can have positive effects on achievement and character development and can serve as a vital link between the school and family.
2. Homework assignments are designed to reinforce classroom instruction, increase understanding and retention, transfer extended classroom instruction, prepare for class discussion and provide curriculum enriched opportunities.
3. Homework enables children to cover topics taught more thoroughly and with greater speed and accuracy and so the activity of self-study becomes a natural complement of teaching.

Types of homework:

1. There are five types of homework such as — Practice (to reinforce skills); Preparation (to get ready for activities); Extension (long-term assignments based on what is happening in class); Application (to apply in new concrete as well as abstract situation) and Creative (to apply knowledge in a creative or imaginative

manner) and Cooperative (to work and learn cooperatively).

Homework and parents

1. Taking an active interest in homework.
2. Ensuring that there is time set aside for homework.
3. Encouraging and supporting students to complete homework.
4. Providing, where possible, a dedicated place and desk or homework and study.
5. Encouraging their children to read and take an interest in current events.
6. Assisting teachers to monitor homework by signing completed homework if requested and being aware of the amount of homework set.
7. Communicating with teachers any concerns about the nature of homework and their children's approach to the homework.
8. Alerting the school to any domestic or co-curricular activities which may need to be taken into consideration when homework is being set or corrected.

Homework and teachers

1. Assign homework regularly and consistently.
2. Make sure students understand the purpose.
3. Make assignment focused and clear.
4. Assign an appropriate amount of homework.
5. Match assignments to style of teaching.
6. Communicate homework policy.
7. Introduce homework planners.
8. Provide choices.
9. Be flexible.
10. Make homework varied.
11. Give help to students as needed.

12. Create assignments that challenge students to think and to integrate.
13. Give homework that makes learning personal.
14. Match assignments to the skills, interest and needs of students.
15. Provide constructive feedback.
16. Do not assign homework as a punishment.

Homework and students

1. Be familiar with the teacher's expectations concerning homework.
2. Demonstrate a commitment to the importance of homework.
3. Complete homework assignments on time, as directed by the teacher.
4. Budget time to complete homework assignment.
5. Use an appropriate study environment (i.e. time, materials, space and conditions).
6. Request help when needed to complete complicated homework assignments.
7. Be responsible for making up missed assignments.
8. Understand the assignment prior to leaving the classroom.
9. Write all assignments in your school designed homework assignment notebook.
10. Share the homework assignment notebook and all teacher communications with parents.
11. Examine daily schedules with parental help and set aside time to do homework.
12. Prioritize homework assignments.
13. Complete long-term homework assignments in manageable steps.
14. Learn from homework, rather than just rushing to finish it.

15. Find out what work has been missed due to absence or any other reason.
16. Make up missed work.
17. Take pride in your homework.

Homework and schools

Schools must have:

1. A Homework policy.
2. After-school academic sessions.
3. The homework centre.
4. The homework hotline.
5. The tutorial programme.
6. The homework guidance centre.

Homework and administrators

1. Review and monitor all teachers' homework guidelines, and make appropriate recommendations to teachers before the guidelines are communicated to the students.
2. Place homework on the agenda at least once a year at their department meetings. This is for the purpose of exchanging ideas and giving each other feedback and information.
3. Assist in the dissemination of the school homework procedures and practices.
4. Review homework procedures and practices periodically at faculty and supervisor meetings.
5. Assist teachers, students and parents in following the school homework practices.
6. Review and monitor all teachers' homework guidelines and makc appropriate recommendations to teachers.
7. Make school-designed assignment notebooks available for purchase at the start of each school year.
8. Ensure that copies of all individual teachers' homework guidelines are on file in either the guidance department or the main office.

9. Monitor the implementation of the policy.
10. Co-ordinate the scheduling of homework among different subjects, if needed.

Homework and researchers

1. In addition to studying homework's overall effectiveness, researchers should examine how variation in assignments might influence their efficacy. One obvious question is whether homework is more effective for some subjects than for others.
2. Researchers should conduct researches on the fact that whether academic performance is a function of increasing homework time at various levels such as elementary, secondary and senior secondary.
3. Studies on the parental involvement should be conducted. For example, is giving parents a formal role in homework affects its utility.
4. Some studies should be conducted regarding individualizing homework assignments, which might have effect on achievement.
5. Some researches should be conducted in which researchers compare a homework feedback strategy (e.g., grading, instruction, or evaluative comments) with a no-feedback approach.
6. Some survey kind of research should be conducted on need and use of homework hotlines to find out effects on academic performance.
7. Research into the costs and benefits of homework for pupils, parents and teachers at primary as well as secondary level.
8. Studies using an experimental design to assess the effectiveness of different homework interventions, such as homework designed to encourage specific types of parental involvement, different types of homework tasks, use of homework planners and different approaches to making and getting feedback.

9. Studies investigating the application of new technology in relation to homework.
10. Research aimed at identifying effective homework practices for lower-achieving pupils and pupils with special educational needs.
11. Studies focusing on the impact of the homework environment and form of task in relation to individual learning styles.
12. Studies concerning the relationship between homework for young (primary age) children and the development of self-regulating learning.
13. Additional studies should "broaden the nature of the criteria used to evaluate the effectiveness of homework. Also, certain intermediate outcomes, such as improved motivation and effective study habits should be used to assess the impact of homework, especially in younger students.
14. The outcomes of homework can also be compared with those of other teaching methods. This will allow the consideration of homework in a wider educational context, thus permitting a more accurate judgement of its value.
15. Homework's effects on achievement and attitudes.

Homework and teacher education programme

1. Homework Education as an intellectual discipline can be introduced.
2. Homework Education can be introduced as a compulsory or optional paper.
3. Every syllabus of teaching subject (Teaching of Mathematics, Physical Science, Life-Science, Social Science, Languages etc.) should have Homework as one of the major contents.
4. Homework as a skill should be given a serious thought.
5. Some modules should be developed to introduce homework as a discipline in Teacher education programme.

In conclusion homework education as a tool and technique has provided some sound theoretical as well as practical learning experiences. It has been rightly called the *instrument* of intellectual development with the wealth of conceptual as well as procedural rules of learning it provides. Its acceptance in the arena of school education has made a significant contribution to the pursuit of making teaching effective and learning creative. If it is used scientifically, it can bring a number of personal qualities essential for personality development.

For the present study, it can be stated categorically that homework as the foremost and powerful tool of learning experience has enough potentiality to enrich the purpose and process of education.

Understandably classroom teaching without adherence to processes of homework would be a chaotic mass of activity. The curricular transactions need various techniques to *define, expound, elucidate, generalise, verify, apply* and even *reflect* upon, the knowledge generated therein. Homework can be used as one of such techniques as it has all the essential ingredients in it to make curriculum transaction possible without any hitch or glitch.

BIBLIOGRAPHY

- Butler, J.A. (1987). *Homework*. NREL, Portland, Oregon.
- Canter, L. and Hauser, L. (1987). *Homework Without Tears*. New York: Perennial Library.
- Cooper, H. (1989). *Homework*. White Plains, NY: Longman.
- Cooper, H. (1994). *The Battle over Homework: An Administrator's Guide to Sound and Effective Policies*. Newbury Park, Calif.: Corwin Press.
- Cooper, H., Lindsay, J.J., Nye, B. and Greathouse, S. (1998). Relationships among attitudes about homework, amount of homework assigned and student achievement. *Journal of Educational Psychology*, 90, 70-83.
- Doyle, M. and Barber, B. (1990). *Homework as a Learning Experience: What Research Says to the Teacher*. 3rd ed. Washington, DC: National Education Association.
- Gill, J.H. (1995). *Learning to Learn: Toward a Philosophy of Education*. New Jersey: Hamilton Press.
- Jha, A.K. (2005). *Nyaya Philosophy: Epistemology and Education*. New Delhi: Standard Publisher (India).
- Klavan, E. (1992). *Taming the Homework Monster*. New York: Poseidon Press.
- Kneller, G.F. (1963). *Foundations of Education*. New York: John Wiley and Sons, Inc.

- Mortimore, P. (1999). *Understanding Pedagogy and Its Impact on Learning*. London: Paul Chapman Publishing Ltd.
- Paulu (1995). *Helping Your Child with Homework: Available on-line.*
- Sharp, C., Keys, W. and Benefield, P. (2001). *Homework: A Review of Recent Research*. Slough: NFER.
- Zentall, S.S. and Goldstein, S. (1999). *Seven Steps to Homework to Success: A Family Guide for Solving Common Homework Problems*. Speciality Press, Inc.
- Rich, D. (1992). *Megaskills: How Families Can Help Children Succeed in School and Beyond*. Boston: Houghton Miffin Company.
- Sonna, L.A. (1990). *The Homework Solution: Getting Kids to do Their Homework*. Charlote, Vermont: Willamson Publishing Co.
- Walberg, H.J. (1991). "Does Homework Help?" *School Community Journal* (1), 13-15.
- http://www.ed.gov/pub/parents/homework/index.html
- http://www.powayusd.sdcoe.k12.ca.us/teachers/bless/homework.htm
- http://www.nea.org/parents/homework.html
- http://www.educationworld.com/clsrm mgmt/index.shtml
- http://www.standards.dfes.gov.uk/homework
- http://www.teachernet.gov.uk
- http://www.gse.harvard.edu
- http://www.pangea.tec.selu.edu
- http://www.students.luther.edu
- http://www.scotia-glenvilleschools.net
- http://www.indianchild.com